GCSE Revision Notes

GCSE Biology

Author
JOHN DOBSON

Series editor **ALAN BREWERTON**

Contents

Life processes and cell activity

Characteristics of living things	4	Cells, tissues, organs and systems	5
Cells	4		

Humans as organisms

Nutrition	9	Senses	18
Food tests	9	Eye	18
Digestion	9	Image detection	18
Digestive system	10	Reflex action, e.g. knee jerk reflex	19
Circulation	11	Reproduction	19
Blood	12	Hormones	20
Respiration	14	Homeostasis	22
Internal respiration - the production of energy within cells	16	Skeleton	24
		Drugs	25
Nervous system	17		

Variation, inheritance and evolution

Variation	27	Genetic engineering	32
Genetics	27	Tissue culture	33
Structure of DNA	30	Cloning	33
Protein synthesis	31	Selective breeding	33
Mutation	31	Evolution	34
Cell division	32		

Microbes, disease and biotechnology

Microbes	37	Food poisoning/spoilage	40
Disease	39	Biotechnology and mankind	41

Living things and their environment

Adaptation and competition	48	Artificial ecosystems	53
Human impact on the environment	49	The carbon cycle	54
		The nitrogen cycle	54
Energy and nutrient transfer	51	Classification of living things	55
Use of ecosystems	53		

Green plants as organisms

Structure of plants	59	Minerals and plant health	62
Photosynthesis	59	Plant hormones	63
Photosynthesis and growth	61	Transport and water relations – transpiration	64
Photosynthesis and assimilation	61		
Transport of minerals and food	61		

Answers 67
Index 69

Life processes and cell activity

Characteristics of living things

Biology – is the science of living things. There are different areas of study:

Zoology – the study of animals
Botany – the study of plants
Microbiology – the study of bacteria, viruses, and fungi.

To be considered as living, all of the following seven characteristics must be present. Some non-living things have some of those characteristics but never all seven, e.g. a car can move, respire and feed (use oxygen to burn fuel) but it is NOT alive!

- **Movement** – living things can move – animals their whole bodies – plants parts of their bodies, e.g. leaves turn towards the sun – flowers can open and close.
- **Respiration** – the release of energy from food – essential to all life – provides energy to carry out life's functions – most organisms use oxygen to respire.
- **Sensitivity** – living things detect and respond to changes in the environment – animals respond quickly by moving – plants usually respond slowly by growing.
- **Feeding** – all living things need food – nutrition – provides energy and other essential substances, e.g. proteins, minerals, etc. – for living things to survive.
- **Excretion** – the removal from the body of waste products, e.g. urea, carbon dioxide, water – from chemical reactions inside cells. *Note* – it is not the removal of waste from digestion, this is called egestion or elimination.
- **Reproduction** – all living things produce young – plants and animals reproduce to make sure their species continue after they die.
- **Growth** – all living things increase in size – usually an increase in number of cells. Animals grow until they become adult – some plants never stop growing.

> Remember these by the phrase **MRS FERG**: movement respiration sensitivity feeding excretion reproduction growth.

Cells

All living things are made up of cells.
Each living thing may be made up of millions of cells or just one cell like the simple animal called amoeba.
All plant and animal cells have these basic parts:

- **Cell membrane** – this is the outside boundary of the cell – it allows certain chemicals to move in and out of the cell.
- **Cytoplasm** – this contains many tiny structures such as mitochondria which keep the cell alive.
- **Mitochondria** – are the energy factories of a cell – these are the structures in the cytoplasm that carry out respiration.
- **Nucleus** – the control centre of a cell – this contains the chemical information needed to make a living thing. Note – human red blood cells do not have nuclei – more space to carry oxygen.

Examiner's tip

It is very important to learn the names of the parts of plant and animal cells.

Plant cells

Plant cells contain all the features of animal cells, but can have extra ones:
- **Cellulose cell wall** – gives the plant cell strength and makes it tough and rigid.
- **Vacuole** – a space filled with water and dissolved chemicals – cell sap. When full of water the plant cell is strong and rigid – said to be **turgid**.
- **Chloroplasts** – contain green **chlorophyll** – this absorbs light – which the plant uses to make food to grow.

> **Examiner's tip**
> Test yourself! Can you draw and label the cells without looking? **This is important!**

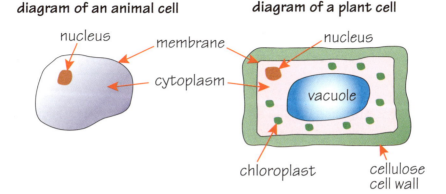

Cells, tissues, organs and systems

Most living things have many different parts – e.g. animals have muscle, blood – plants have seeds, leaves, etc.

The cells of these different parts have structures that make them specialised to do certain functions.

Cells can form:
- **Tissues** – specialised groups of identical cells – all have the same function.
- **Organs** – many tissues grouped together – form structure with specific functions.
- **Systems** – a lot of organs grouped together – for specific functions.
- **Organisms** – a lot of systems grouped together.

Examples

- **Muscle tissue** – contains lots of identical muscle cells.
- **Lung** – an organ containing the tissues – muscle + blood + nerve + other tissues.
- **Respiratory system** – containing the organs – lung + trachea + diaphragm + ribs + muscles.
- **Glandular tissue** – a collection of glandular cells (producing enzymes, etc.).
- **Stomach** – an organ containing the tissues – glandular + nerve + muscle + blood + other tissues.
- **Digestive system** – a system which includes – mouth + oesophagus + stomach + intestines + other organs.
- **Xylem tissue** – lots of xylem cells (transport water in plants) – xylem cells form vessels.
- **Leaf** – an organ which contains the tissues – xylem + phloem + mesophyll + epidermis.

> **Examiner's tip**
> You may be asked to relate structure and function.

> Try to learn the names of some cells, organs and systems.

Cell division - mitosis

All cells (except human red blood cells) have **nuclei**.

A nucleus contains:
- **Chromosomes** – contain **genes**.
- **Genes** – control all features of all living things – there are hundreds of genes on each chromosome.

Living things have pairs of chromosomes – e.g. each human cell has 23 pairs, which means 46 chromosomes in every nucleus of every cell in your body.

For every characteristic there is a pair of genes – e.g. one pair of genes controls your eye colour, another pair your height.

Different genes for the same characteristic are called <u>alleles</u>. The genes in a pair do not have to be the same – your genes for eye colour may be one brown and one blue.

New cells are produced by the process of **cell division**.

All your body cells were produced from one cell – formed when a sperm fertilised an ovum.

This cell divided as follows:

$$1 \rightarrow 2 \rightarrow 4 \rightarrow 8 \rightarrow 16 \rightarrow 32 \rightarrow 64,$$ etc. producing millions of cells.

These cells may be damaged and die – they need replacing – you also have to grow – new cells are produced by cell division.

All the chromosomes are copied and every cell gets a nucleus with copies of all the original chromosomes within it.

Producing sex cells - meiosis

- Involves reproductive organs only – testes and ovaries of animals – anthers and ovaries of plants.
- Chromosomes pair – cells contain like pairs of chromosomes.
- Like pairs are separated.
- Cell divides.
- Cell divides again.
- 4 new nuclei produced.

When human sex cells join together the original number of chromosomes is restored – i.e. sperm (**23** chromosomes) + ovum (**23** chromosomes) fuse together to produce the first human cell (zygote) with **46** chromosomes.

> Watch mitosis on CD-ROM or video if you can. This will help you to understand what is happening.

> Watch meiosis on CD-ROM or video if you can. This will help you to understand what is happening.

Cell membranes

These are made from protein and fat (lipid).
Membranes allow certain chemicals to move in and out of the cell. Movement of molecules occurs by **diffusion**.

Diffusion

- Diffusion is the movement of molecules from a higher to a lower concentration.
- In living things it occurs in solution — even gases must dissolve first.
- Molecules pass through cell membranes — these have some control over what enters and leaves a cell.
- Large molecules diffuse more **slowly** than small molecules.
- The greater the concentration difference the faster diffusion occurs.

Examples of diffusion include:
- Oxygen enters blood in alveoli — dissolves in mucus first.
- Food enters villi in ileum.
- Carbon dioxide enters leaf through stomatal pore — then leaf cells.

Osmosis

- This is a special case of diffusion — of **water**.
- Diffusion of water from area of high concentration of water (high water potential) to area of low concentration of water (low water potential).
- Semi permeable membrane allows water across but may not allow solute molecules to pass.

> **Examiner's tip**
> Learn your teacher's definition of osmosis.

Active Transport

- Movement against a concentration gradient can occur — cells use energy to pull molecules across membranes — **active transport** — example of membrane selectivity.
- Occurs in: digestive system — villi — to absorb food molecules
  kidneys — nephrons — to reabsorb glucose from filtrate
  plant roots — root hairs — absorb minerals

Questions

LIFE PROCESSES AND CELL ACTIVITY

1 What is the study of plants called? _____

2 What is the study of animals called? _____

3 What is responding to changes in the environment called? _____

4 What is the release of energy from food called? _____

5 What is removing waste products from the body called?_____

6 What is removing the waste from digestion called? _____

7 What is producing new members of the species called? _____

8 What is increasing in size called? _____

9 Which gas is commonly used in respiration?_____

10 Which characteristic of living things is responsible for producing energy?

_____

11 What is the function of mitochondria?_____

12 Which phrase helps you to remember 7 characteristics of living things?

_____

13 What are the fluid contents of a cell called? _____

14 Which part of a cell controls its functions? _____

15 What is the outside of a plant cell called? _____

16 In which part of the plant cell is chlorophyll found? _____

17 Which part of the plant cell is filled with cell sap? _____

18 What is a group of cells carrying out the same function called? _____

19 What is a group of tissues carrying out one function called? _____

20 What is a group of organs carrying out one function called? _____

21 What do a group of organ systems make up? _____

22 What features do plant cells have that animal cells do not? _____

_____

23 What is a neuron an example of? _____

24 What is the heart an example of?_____

25 What is the stomach an example of? _____

26 What is diffusion?_____

_____

27 What is active transport? _____

_____

Humans as organisms

Nutrition

Humans need seven types of chemical compound in their diet:

- **Carbohydrate** – e.g. starch, glucose, sugar, glycogen – used for **energy**.
- **Protein** – made from amino acids – used for growth and repair of cells – enzymes and some hormones are proteins.
- **Fat** – made from fatty acids and glycerol – used for energy – part of cell membranes.
- **Minerals** – like iron – in haemoglobin – red blood cells – lack of = anaemia, and calcium in bones and teeth – lack of = rickets.
- **Vitamins** like C – lack of = scurvy, D – for bones and teeth – lack of = rickets, and A – lack of = night blindness.
- **Water** – solvent for all chemicals in body.
- **Fibre** – roughage – helps food travel along digestive system.

Food tests

Simple experiments can be used to identify food types. The following are tests for food:

- **Starch** – add **iodine** solution – do not heat – blue-black colour = starch – any other colour = no starch.
- **Protein** – Biuret test – use **Biuret** reagent – purple ring/purple colour = protein.
- **Glucose** or simple sugars – **Benedicts** reagent – add Benedicts and heat – brick red precipitate = a lot of glucose – orange colour = less glucose – yellow colour = less glucose still – green colour = tiny amount of glucose – blue colour = no glucose.
- **Fats** – add alcohol – dissolves fat – then add water – white/cloudiness = fat present in food
  or
  rub food on paper – grease stain – paper becomes translucent = fat present.

Digestion

Carbohydrate (starch), protein and fat are insoluble in water.

Digestion breaks down large, insoluble, complex molecules into smaller, simpler, soluble molecules.
Enzymes carry out digestion – speed up chemical changes – they are catalysts.

Digestive system

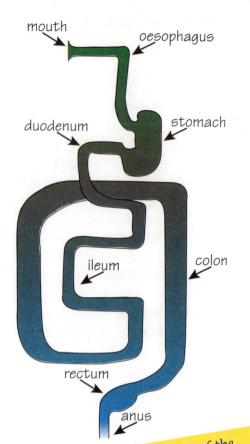

Mouth

- **Salivary carbohydrase** (amylase) digests starch to maltose (glucose molecule pairs) and glucose.
- Saliva lubricates food.
- Makes it easy to swallow.
- Chewing increases surface area for enzyme to work on.

Oesophagus

- Gullet – food squeezed – **peristalsis** – how food moves inside the gut.
- Peristalsis – gut has circular and longitudinal muscles – circular muscles squeeze food – longitudinal muscles expand gut again.

Stomach

- **Hydrochloric acid** kills germs – bacteria, fungi, viruses.
- Creates best conditions for enzyme – pH2.
- **Gastric protease** – digests protein into peptides into amino acids.

Remember the names of the organs of the digestive system with the word MOSDICRA: mouth oesophagus stomach duodenum ileum colon rectum anus.

Duodenum

- **Bile** – made in the **liver** – stored in **gall bladder**.
- Bile emulsifies fats – breaks them into tiny droplets of fat – **bile is not an enzyme** – gives a large surface area for enzymes to work on.
- Digestive juice from **pancreas** – contains enzymes and neutralises acid from stomach – enzymes act best in slightly alkaline conditions.
- **Pancreatic lipase** – digests fat into fatty acids and glycerol – **pancreatic carbohydrase** and **protease** act as above.

Ileum

Note duodenum + ileum = small intestine.

- Enzymes complete digestion.
- **Intestinal carbohydrase, protease** and **lipase** digest foods as above.
- Soluble, simple food absorbed into bloodstream.
- Adapted for diffusion of small molecules – large surface area – villi.
- Thin, moist, semi-permeable cell membranes – allow diffusion of food into blood.
- Active transport – for some molecules – energy used by cells to absorb food molecules.

Large intestine - colon
- Water is reabsorbed – into blood – important – prevents dehydration.
- Indigestible food remains – **faeces**.

Rectum
- Stores faeces until they are eliminated – through **anus**.

Circulation

Heart

Has four chambers:

- <mark>Right atrium</mark> – receives blood from body via **inferior vena cava** and from **head** via **superior vena cava** – pumps blood into →
- <mark>Right ventricle</mark> – pumps blood to **lungs** via **pulmonary artery**.
- <mark>Left atrium</mark> – receives blood from **lungs** via **pulmonary vein** – pumps blood into →
- <mark>Left ventricle</mark> – most muscular chamber – pumps blood all around body – via **aorta**.

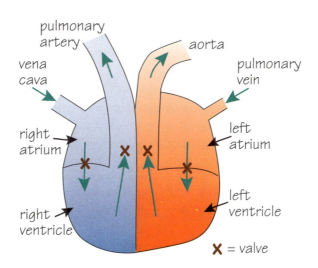

Heart – simple diagram

Four valves:
- One between right atrium and ventricle.
- One between left atrium and ventricle.
- One at exit of right ventricle.
- One at exit of left ventricle.

Blood flow

From major vein (vena cava) – right atrium – valve – right ventricle – valve – pulmonary artery – lungs (one circulation system) – pulmonary vein – left atrium – valve – left ventricle – valve – aorta (main artery) – body (second circulation system).

The valves stop the blood flowing in the wrong direction.

Blood vessels

Arteries

- Thick walls – elastic – have muscle.
- Need to withstand high pressure.
- Carry blood **away** from the heart.
- Deep in the body for protection.

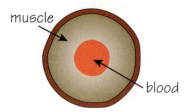

Veins

- Thinner walls than arteries.
- Have **valves** to keep blood flowing towards the heart.
- Near muscles to help squeeze blood back to the heart – e.g. calf muscles squeeze blood up from leg.

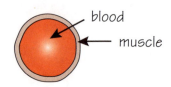

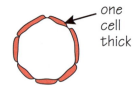

Capillaries

- Very thin – walls one cell thick.
- Leak tissue fluid – dissolved food and oxygen is carried to cells.
- Exchange food, oxygen, carbon dioxide, waste, cell products – between blood and organs.
- Capillary exchange mechanisms are present in all organs – e.g. ileum – villi, lung – alveoli, kidney – nephron.
- Provide very large surface area for diffusion.

Blood

Contains **red cells, white cells, platelets** and **plasma**.

Red cells

- Carry oxygen in haemoglobin.
- Oxygen + haemoglobin → oxyhaemoglobin – in lungs.

- Oxyhaemoglobin → oxygen + haemoglobin – in all body tissues.
- No nucleus – more room to carry oxygen.
- Made in bone marrow – live approximately 120 days.
- Poisoned by **carbon monoxide** – person suffocates from lack of oxygen.
- Biconcave shape – larger surface area – absorbing O_2

Blood groups

- Four major human blood groups – A, AB, B and O.
- Sub-divided into two other groups – rhesus –ve and rhesus +ve.
- Major blood transfusions – must match groups exactly.
- Minor blood transfusions – rhesus must match – O can be used for any person = universal donor.
- AB = universal recipient – minor transfusions only.

yes = transfusion
no = no transfusion

	donor blood			
patient's blood group	A	B	AB	O
A	yes	no	no	yes
B	no	yes	no	yes
AB	yes	yes	yes	yes
O	no	no	no	yes

White cells

- Have nuclei.
- Made in bone marrow.
- **T lymphocytes** – have **antibodies** on cell membrane – destroys foreign cells.
- **B lymphocytes** – divide to produce clones – cells produce **antibodies** – enter plasma and destroy foreign cells.
- **Phagocytes** – defend the body against any invaders – e.g. bacteria, viruses – detect invaders and ingest (eat) them – can alter shape – like Amoeba – squeeze through capillary walls and patrol inter cellular spaces – therefore not confined to blood.
- **Antibodies** – made by B cells – lymph glands – destroy microbes and foreign tissue.
- **Antitoxins** – destroy poisons produced by microbes.
- **Immune system memory** – once you have had a disease you are immune – **vaccinations** trigger immune memory – **boosters** needed as a reminder for some diseases.

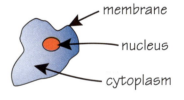

Note you get lots of colds because the virus is different each time.

Immunity (see disease section)

- People immunised with vaccines – produce antibodies – ongoing immunity – called **active immunity** – is active all the time – may need booster vaccinations, e.g. polio.
- Antibodies can be injected directly – in response to a dangerous infection, e.g. rabies, tetanus – this combats the disease but does not last – called **passive immunity**.

Platelets

- Made in bone marrow – from parts of much larger cells.
- React to cell damage/air.
- Produce fibres to trap red blood cells and **clot the blood**.

Plasma

- Liquid part of blood.
- Carries all cells.
- Dissolves **carbon dioxide** – carries it to lungs.
- Carries dissolved **food** from small intestine to liver and all cells.
- Carries **urea** from liver to kidneys.

Respiration

Breathing in:
- Ribs move up and out – by external intercostal muscles contracting.
- **Diaphragm** muscles contract – diaphragm moves down – flattens.
- Volume of chest increases.
- Pressure decreases (Boyle's Law – Physics) – to below air pressure.
- Air pressure forces air into the lungs.

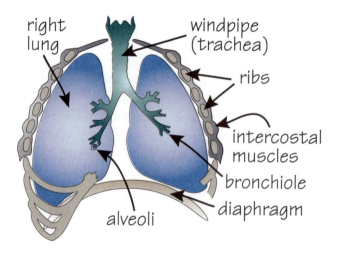

System includes: trachea, bronchi, bronchioles, alveoli.

Cillia

- Cilia clean airways – found in bronchi.
- Cilia deactivated by smoking.
- Lungs clog up – cannot clean themselves.
- Stopping smoking allows cilia to recover.

Alveoli

- Air sacs – provide a large surface area for gas exchange.
- Thin – only 1 or 2 cells separate oxygen from blood.
- Moist – lined with mucus – dissolves oxygen.
- Semi-permeable membranes – allow diffusion of gases.
- Good blood supply – capillaries cover alveoli – gases oxygen and carbon dioxide exchanged.

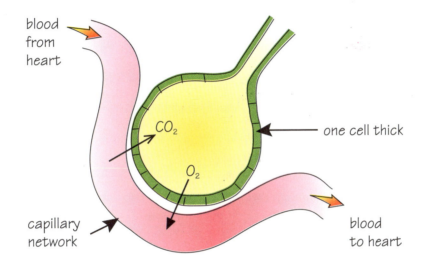

Inhaled and exhaled air

	inhaled air	exhaled air
oxygen	21%	16%
nitrogen	78%	78%
carbon dioxide	0.03%	4%
other	1%	1%

- Air loses approximately ¼ of its oxygen in the lungs – blood gains oxygen.
- Air gains carbon dioxide in the lungs – blood loses carbon dioxide.
- Both oxygen and carbon dioxide are soluble in mucus in the lungs.
- No change in % nitrogen – nitrogen is **insoluble** at normal atmospheric pressure.

Note
- Scuba diving – nitrogen dissolves at high pressure – high pressure under water – danger of 'the bends' if surfacing too quickly – this is when nitrogen bubbles form in the blood – like taking the top off a pop bottle.
- Safety – surface slowly or use decompression chambers.
- Also nitrogen narcosis – like being drunk – causes disorientation problems for divers.
- Safety – don't use nitrogen – use oxygen/helium mixture – no disorientation – though talk like Donald Duck – but does not stop the problems with surfacing too quickly.

Internal respiration – the production of energy within cells

Aerobic respiration

You must learn these equations!

Glucose + oxygen → carbon dioxide + water + energy

$$C_6H_{12}O_6 + 6O_2 \rightarrow 6CO_2 + 6H_2O + energy$$

- Glucose carried in plasma.
- Oxygen carried in red blood cells.
- Cell cytoplasm – **mitochondria** – contains enzymes for respiration.
- Carbon dioxide carried away by plasma.
- Water – **metabolic water** – important source of water in desert animals.

Energy is used for:
- Making molecules, e.g. proteins from amino acids.
- Muscle contraction.
- Heat production in birds and mammals – constant body temperature – homeostasis.
- **Active transport** – diffusion of small molecules against a diffusion gradient, e.g. food in the ileum, glucose in the kidney nephron, minerals in plant roots.

Exercise

- Muscles respire **aerobically** – for a short time – they rapidly run out of oxygen.
- **Anaerobic** respiration starts.
- Glucose broken into two molecules of **lactic acid** – energy is released so muscles can continue to work.
- Aerobic respiration occurs when enough oxygen in cell – anaerobic respiration when not enough oxygen in cell.
- **Lactic acid** builds up as anaerobic respiration continues.
- Build up of lactic acid causes muscle fatigue.
- **Oxygen debt** results – oxygen needed to remove all lactic acid after exercise.

- Anaerobic respiration produces much less energy than aerobic.
- Carbon dioxide is not produced by anaerobic respiration in muscles.

Glucose → lactic acid + energy

Remember this equation

- Relationship between heart rate, breathing rate and exercise.
- Increase exercise – increase heart rate and volume of blood pumped by heart on each beat, i.e. the stroke volume.
- Increase exercise – increase breathing rate and depth of breathing.
- Increases supply of oxygen and glucose to muscles.
- Increases removal of carbon dioxide from muscle cells –
- Increases uptake of oxygen from lungs.
- Increases removal of carbon dioxide from lungs.
- Regular exercise improves fitness – recovery rate from exercise improves.
- Regular exercise increases the muscles' tolerance to lactic acid so it takes longer for them to become tired.

Nervous system

Central nervous system – CNS

- Brain.
- Spinal cord.

Neurons

- Cell body – contains nucleus – controls neuron.
- Axon – can be very long – over a metre – transmits chemical impulse along its length – insulated by myelin sheath.
- Dendron – branching fibres – pass impulse onto next neuron or make muscle/gland respond.

Sensory
- Transmits messages from receptors to CNS.
- Cell body is situated on one side of axon.

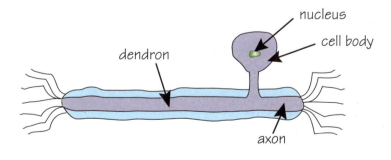

direction of impulse

HUMANS AS ORGANISMS

Motor
- Transmits messages from CNS to effectors – i.e. muscles, glands and organs.
- Cell body in line with axon.

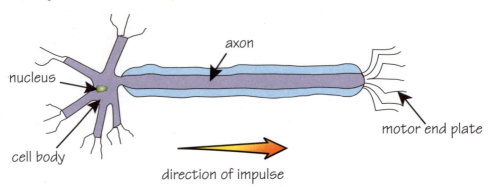

Relay
- Mostly in CNS – transmits messages between sensory and motor neurons.

Senses
- Hearing and balance – the **ear**.
- Sight – the **eye**.
- Smell – the **nose**.
- Taste – bitter, sweet, salt and sour – the **tongue**.
- Touch, pain pressure and temperature senses – the **skin**.

The CNS works in this order:

STIMULUS → RECEPTOR → CO-ORDINATOR → EFFECTOR → RESPONSE

Eye

- **Cornea** – transparent.
- **Sclera** – tough – protection.
- **Iris** – muscles control size of **pupil** – large in dim light – small in bright light.
- **Pupil** – hole for light to enter eye.
- **Retina** – light-sensitive cells – **rods** for dim light – **cones** for colour.
- **Lens** – shape controlled by **suspensory ligaments and ciliary muscle**.
- **Optic nerve** – takes nerve impulses from retina to brain.

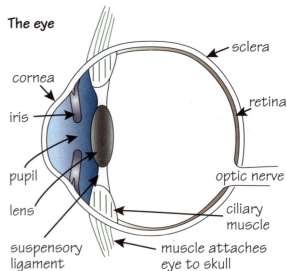

Image detection
- Light enters eye – cornea and lens focus light – lens thin for distant – relaxed ciliary muscles – thick for near objects – contracted ciliary muscles – light focused on retina.
- Receptor cells – send message via optic nerve to brain – brain interprets image.

Reflex action, e.g. knee jerk reflex

- **Receptor** detects stimulus, e.g. tap on knee.
- Sends message (impulse) – sensory nerve to **CNS** – co-ordinator, in this case = spinal cord.
- **Synapse** – gap between sensory neuron and relay neuron – chemical messenger crosses gap – neurotransmitter – passes impulse to relay neuron.
- **Synapse** – gap between relay and motor neuron – neurotransmitter – passes impulse to motor neuron.
- **Motor neuron** carries impulse to effector – in this case = thigh muscle.
- **Effector** produces response – in this case = leg moves forward. Effectors make muscles move or glands secrete, e.g. saliva at the smell of food.

Examiner's tip

Important — You must be able to analyse any given situation in terms of **stimulus receptor co-ordinator effector response**.

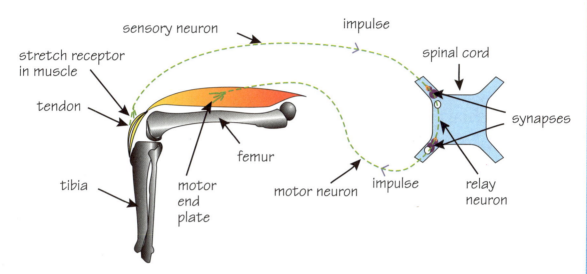

Reproduction

Male reproductive organs

- **Testes** – produce sperm and male hormone – testosterone – check testes for lumps – cancer – in under 35s – easy to treat successfully if caught early.
- **Sperm tubes** – vas deferens – transport sperm and semen to urethra.
- **Urethra** – tube in centre of penis – conducts semen and sperm into female.
- **Penis** – contains erectile tissue – allows penis to become erect – enables sexual intercourse to occur.
- **Scrotum** – contains testes – outside body – kept cooler for optimum sperm production.

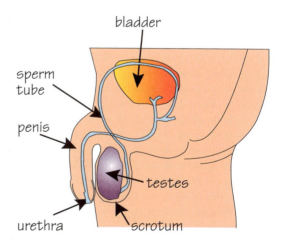

Female reproductive organs

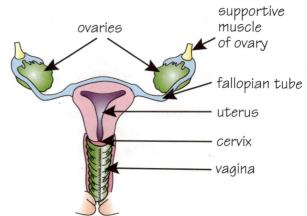

- **Ovaries** – produce mature ova and female hormones – oestrogen and progesterone.
- **Oviducts** – fallopian tubes – transport ovum from ovary to uterus – fertilisation occurs here.
- **Uterus** – very muscular, pushes baby out at birth – protects the developing embryo – placenta feeds, provides oxygen and removes waste from embryo.
- **Cervix** – opening to uterus – smear tests for cervical cancer – treatable if caught early.
- **Vagina** – birth canal – also sperm deposited here during sexual intercourse.

Menstrual cycle

- Day 1 to 5 – lining is lost from the uterus – called a period.
- Day 6 to 13 – lining of the uterus thickens ready for an embryo.
- Day 14 – ovulation occurs – a mature egg is released from an ovary.
- Day 15 – ovum travels along fallopian tube – it may be fertilised by *one* sperm – usually fertilisation does not occur and the ovum dies.
- Day 16 to 21 – hormone levels in woman's body start to alter (see hormones).
- Day 22 to 28 – lining of the uterus stops developing.
- Day 29 = 1 – lining of the uterus breaks down and is passed out of the vagina – this is a period – the cycle starts again.
- If an ovum is fertilised on day 14 – the lining of the uterus helps to form the placenta – feeds and protects the embryo.
- No more periods will occur nor eggs released until after the baby is born.
- 2 ova + 2 sperm = *non-identical twins*.
- 1 ovum + 1 sperm – first embryo divides in two – *identical twins*.

Hormones

Control and co-ordinate many body processes.

Blood sugar

This is monitored and controlled by the pancreas.

Glucose level in blood too high:
- **Pancreas** releases *hormone insulin* into blood.
- **Insulin** picked up by *liver* from blood.
- **Liver cells** – take glucose from blood – convert to *glycogen* – stored.
- Blood sugar returns to normal.

Glucose level in blood too low:
- **Pancreas** releases hormone glucagon into blood.
- **Glucagon** picked up by liver from blood.
- **Liver cells** – convert glycogen to glucose – glucose released into blood.
- Blood sugar returns to normal.

Menstrual cycle

Controlled by hormones from the pituitary gland in the brain and the ovaries.

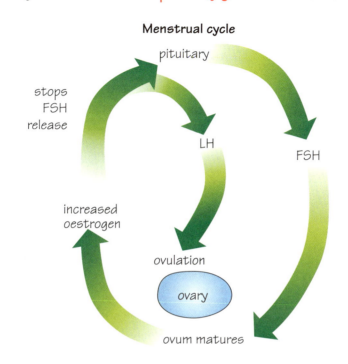

Draw a diagram like this to help you remember blood sugar control.

- Day 1 – 5 – period occurs.
- Day 6 – 13 – uterus lining thickens – caused by oestrogen and progesterone from ovary – prepares to receive fertilised ovum – ovum maturing – caused by hormone FSH from pituitary.
- Day 14 – ovulation – caused by hormone LH from pituitary.
- Day 15–28 – embryo implants – or if NOT pregnant, uterus lining stops developing – lack of hormones.
- Day 29 = day 1 – uterus lining shed – period – if not pregnant.

Fertility treatment

FSH given – stimulates ovum development in ovaries – more than one ova may mature – problem – multiple births.

Be prepared to discuss the benefits and problems.

Contraception

Oestrogen given – inhibits FSH production by pituitary – no eggs mature – none released – problem – body thinks it's pregnant – side effects – weight gain – possible sickness – take with medical supervision only.

HUMANS AS ORGANISMS

Water balance

Hormone – **anti-diuretic hormone** – **ADH** – produced by **pituitary gland** – see **homeostasis**.

Homeostasis

This is the control of the body's internal environment.

Excretion

The removal of waste products produced by cells.

Lungs

- Remove carbon dioxide – waste product of respiration.
- Some water lost – breath is moist.

Liver

- Excess amino acids broken down – urea formed + carbohydrate.
- Carbohydrate – energy source – stored as glycogen or used in respiration.
- Urea enters blood and removed by kidneys.

Kidneys

- Two bean shaped structures.
- Filter the blood – glomerulus – higher blood pressure.
- All small substances removed, e.g. water, urea, salt and glucose.
- Glucose is needed by body – all glucose reabsorbed by nephron by **active transport** – cells use energy to do this.
- Some salt – sodium and chloride ions – reabsorbed.
- Water – see osmoregulation below.
- Urea, salt ions and water are excreted – urine – stored in the bladder – eliminated as necessary.

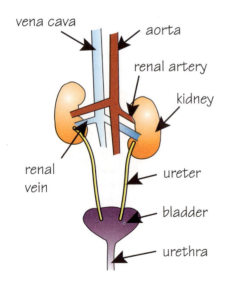

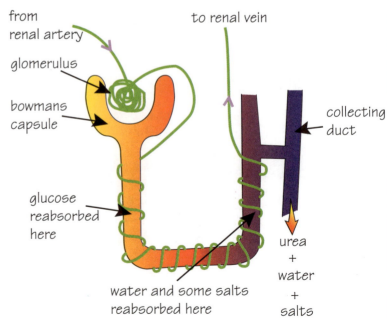

Kidney failure

- Kidney machine used to keep patient alive – performs function of kidney.
- Dialysis usually performed three times a week.
- Transplant performed when donor kidney is available.
- Organ donor registry scheme – no longer need donor cards.

> Be prepared to evaluate the advantages and disadvantages of kidney machines and transplants.

Osmoregulation - water regulation - the most important job of the kidney

Brain monitors blood concentration.

Blood is too concentrated – not enough water:	**Blood too dilute – too much water:**
<ul><li>Feeling of thirst – drink water.</li><li>**Pituitary produces more ADH** – travels in blood.</li><li>Makes **kidney nephron more permeable** to reabsorb water back into blood.</li><li>**Urine is more concentrated** – less water is lost.</li><li>Blood returns to normal.</li></ul>	<ul><li>**Pituitary gland releases less ADH.**</li><li>**Kidney nephron is less permeable to water.**</li><li>Urine is more dilute – more water is lost.</li><li>Blood returns to normal.</li></ul>

Adrenaline - the 'flight or fight' hormone

- Produced by adrenal glands above kidneys.
- Prepares body for action.
- Increases respiration in muscle cells – more energy.
- Increases breathing rate – more oxygen.
- Increases release of glucose from liver – more food for cells.
- Dilates blood capillaries in limb muscles – more blood to cells.
- Muscles ready for action.
- Nervous system ready for action.
- Constricts blood vessels in gut – causes 'butterflies in stomach'.
- Resources in body diverted to where needed.

Skin

- Sweating – loses heat, water, salt ions and some urea; temperature control.

HUMANS AS ORGANISMS

Temperature control

- **Stimulus** – *environment too hot.*
- Thermoregulatory centre in brain monitors core body temperature.
- Skin temperature *receptor* – impulses in sensory nerve – to brain (co-ordinator).
- Brain sends messages – nerve impulse and hormone – to skin – blood vessels dilate (get wider – vasodilation) – more blood to skin surface – more heat lost.

    Note – capillary muscles = *effector* – dilating = *response*.

- Also message to sweat glands – sweat on skin – liquid evaporates – cool down.

- **Stimulus** – *environment too cold*
- Brain and skin detect.
- Skin blood vessels constrict (vasoconstriction) – less blood to skin – less heat lost.
- Brain – message to muscles to shiver – respiration releases energy as heat.

Skeleton

The skeleton has three functions:
- Support of body and facilitating movement.
- Protection, e.g. brain protected by skull.
- Manufacture of blood cells and platelets.

Bones of the arm are humerus, radius and ulna.
- Hip bone = pelvis.
- Thigh bone = femur.
- Shoulder blade = scapula.

Arm movement involves:
- Radius and ulna – lower arm.
- Humerus – upper arm.
- Humerus and ulna form elbow joint.
- Humerus and scapula form shoulder joint.

Synovial joints

- Synovial fluid lubricates moving joints.
- Joints held together by ligaments.
- Ends of bones covered with cartilage – protects bone.
- Ball and socket joints at hip and shoulder.
- Hinge joints at knee and elbow.

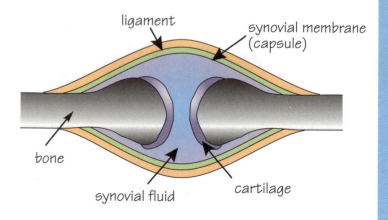

Arthritis

- Affects joints – cartilage wears away.
- Movement becomes very painful.
- Can replace joint with artificial one – e.g. hip replacement – lasts 10–15 years only – a second operation may be needed.
- Use carbon fibre for socket and metal alloy for head of femur.
- New technique – replaces end of bone only – allows operation to be performed more times in a person's lifetime – techniques advancing all the time.

> Be prepared to discuss the advantages and disadvantages of joint replacement therapy.

Drugs

These are any chemicals that enter the body and have an effect. They can be:

- Useful – e.g. paracetamol – pain relief, antibiotics – kill microbes.
- Harmful – e.g. nicotine – dependence on cigarettes, alcohol – liver problems.
- Very dangerous – e.g. paracetamol – can be fatal with overdose, heroin – addictive, cocaine – addictive – withdrawal problems – very hard to quit.

Drug misuse

The effect of drugs on a person depends upon the person's state of health and mind. The same drug can affect two different people in very different ways.

Solvents

- Seriously affect behaviour, drug is in control.
- Damage liver, lungs and brain.
- Most deaths caused by inhaling vomit when unconscious.

Tobacco

- Nicotine is addictive – affects blood pressure – calms people down – hard to give up.
- Other chemicals in cigarettes cause cancer of throat, lung, stomach.
- Breathing problems – emphysema, bronchitis – damaged cilia.
- Carbon monoxide – in smoke – blood carries less oxygen – raises blood pressure.
- Heart and blood vessels affected – heart disease, artery disease.

Alcohol

- Affects nervous system – small amounts – mild anaesthetic – slows reactions.
- Larger amounts – affects motor control – movement, speech – person is not in control.
- Very large amounts – coma – unconsciousness can follow – can be fatal.
- Heavy drinking for a long time causes severe liver damage – cirrhosis – death will result – brain damage also.

Questions

HUMANS AS ORGANISMS

1   Which three types of food need digesting? _____

2   How does food travel along the digestive system? _____

3   What are the two functions of the acid in the stomach?_____

   _____

4   What is the function of bile? _____

   _____

5   What is the function of a protease? _____

6   Which chamber of the heart pumps blood to the lungs? _____

7   Which chamber of the heart pumps blood around the body? _____

8   Why do arteries have thick muscular walls? _____

   _____

9   Why do veins have valves? _____

   _____

10   What is the function of red blood cells? _____

11   Name three things carried by blood plasma._____

12   Where in the lungs does diffusion take place? _____

13   Which type of respiration uses oxygen? _____

14   Which type of respiration does not use oxygen? _____

15   What is the order of events in any nervous response?

   _____

16   Name three parts of a synovial joint. _____

17   Which hormone reduces blood sugar levels? _____

18   Which hormone raises blood sugar levels?_____

19   Which hormone causes ova to mature?_____

20   Which hormone causes ovulation?_____

21   What happens to excess amino acids in the body? _____

   _____

22   What effect does ADH have on the kidney nephron?_____

   _____

23   Where does fertilisation occur?_____

24   On which day of the menstrual cycle is an ovum likely to be released from an ovary?

   _____

Variation, inheritance and evolution

Variation

Living organisms look like their parents. They have similar characteristics. This is because their parents passed on information in their **genes** when sexual reproduction took place. Genes are carried on **chromosomes**.

The parents pass on equal amounts of information to their offspring. **Genes control all the characteristics of all living things**.

Differences in living things of the same species are caused by:
- Different genes passed on from parents – these are genetic differences.
- The **environment** – these are the conditions in which a living thing develops.
- **Continuous variation** – gradual differences in characteristics, i.e. height.
- **Discontinuous variation** – abrupt differences, i.e. ear lobes attached or not, tongue roller or not.

Genetics

This is the study of how **information** is passed on from one generation to the next.

You must learn the names used in genetics!

- Different genes control different **characteristics** – alleles are different forms of a gene.
  Genes are found in pairs – like pairs = **homozygous**, e.g. BB = black fur, bb = brown fur.
- Unlike pairs = **heterozygous**, e.g. Bb = black fur.
- **Genotype** = the pair of genes/alleles for a characteristic, e.g. BB or Bb or bb.
- **Phenotype** = what the characteristic is, e.g. black fur or brown fur.
- **F1** = first generation after a genetic cross.
- **F2** = second generation.

Different characteristics may be due to different genes or different conditions in the environment.

Environment

The environment can affect how living things grow – not enough food or nutrients – animals and plants will not grow as well – too much competition in one place – animals or plants may be stunted in development.
The opposite could also be true if there was very little competition.

Chromosomes

Genes are found on **chromosomes**. Chromosomes are in pairs in all body cells of all animals and most plants.

In humans there are 46 chromosomes – 23 pairs in all body cells – every cell in your body has **all** of the genes that carry the information to make another copy of you.

Chromosomes are made from the chemical called DNA – it has the unique property that it can replicate itself exactly – when your cells divide they can produce exact copies of your chromosomes and therefore your genes.

Heredity

- Genes are passed on from one generation to the next.
- Every living thing must reproduce in order to survive – means passing on genes to the next generation.
- A living thing is a biological success if it leaves copies of its genes in its offspring before it dies.
- The more copies of its genes it leaves, the bigger a success.

Human beings

- Human cells have 46 chromosomes in their cell nuclei.
- When an ovum is fertilised to produce a baby, the baby must also have 46 chromosomes.
- Sex cells like sperm and ova have 23 chromosomes – sperm and the ovum contribute equally to the embryo.
- 23 chromosomes from sperm + 23 chromosomes from ovum = 46 chromosomes in embryo.

The inheritance of sex

- Humans have sex chromosomes called X and Y.
- Females have two X chromosomes (XX).
- Males have one X and one Y (XY).
- When sex cells are produced these sex chromosomes separate and end up in different cells.
- All ova will have X chromosomes only.
- There are two types of sperm – one with a Y chromosome – one with an X chromosome.

Genetics of cystic fibrosis

- Caused by a **recessive gene**.
- Breathing and digestion problems.
- Sufferers have a shorter life expectancy.
- Adults can be normal but carry a recessive cystic gene.
- Condition usually runs in families but may miss generations.

Genetic problems are a good chance of full marks – make sure you know how to do them! Set them out clearly.

Let N = normal dominant gene and c = recessive cystic gene.

parents: (Nc) (carrier)   x   (Nc) (carrier)
sex cells: N or c   N or c

	N	c
N	NN	Nc
c	Nc	cc

offspring: 1 NN   2Nc   1cc
              normal   carrier   cystic fibrosis
              25% chance   50% chance   25% chance

Conclusion: Two carrier parents have a 25% (1 in 4) chance of having a cystic child.

Huntington's chorea

Caused by a **dominant gene**.

- Affects the nervous system – loss of motor and sensory function and quickly leads to death.
- Person will be perfectly normal until about 35 to 45 years of age.
- Then develops Huntington's Chorea and becomes seriously ill and dies.
- By this time may have had a family and passed the gene on to their children.

Let H = the dominant Huntington gene and n = normal recessive gene.

parents: (Hn) x (nn)
sex cells: H or n   n or n

offspring: 2 Hn   2 nn
      Huntington's chorea normal
      50%   50%

	H	n
n	Hn	nn
n	Hn	nn

Conclusion: A Huntington's parent has a 50% (1 : 2) chance of passing the disease on to their children.

Sickle cell anaemia

- Caused by a **recessive gene**.
- Disease is inherited from both parents who carry the gene.
- Name comes from the shape of the red blood cells that the disease produces.

Let N = normal red cells and s = sickle cells. N is dominant and s is recessive.

Parents: (Ns) x (Ns)
sex cells: N or s   N or s

offspring: 1 NN   2 Ns   1 ss
      normal carrier sickle cell anaemia
      25%   50%   25%

	N	s
N	NN	Ns
s	Ns	ss

Conclusion: Two carriers of sickle cell genes have a 25% (1 in 4) chance of having a child with sickle cell anaemia.

Sickle cell disease is fatal. The gene is still in the population of people who live where there is malaria because people who are carriers of the gene have a greater resistance to malaria than normal people. So in malaria areas:

NN – catch malaria and die,   Ns – survive,   ss – die of sickle cell anaemia.

Sex linked conditions

- Caused by X chromosome having extra DNA not represented on Y chromosome.
- **Muscular dystrophy** – muscle wastage – fatal by adolescence.
- **Haemophilia** – cannot make Factor 8 protein which clots the blood.
- **Colour blindness** – cannot distinguish blue/green or red/green – cone development!
- These conditions are inherited from the mother – she carries a recessive gene on one of her X chromosomes.
- Father's X chromosome has a normal gene but Y chromosome has gene missing, e.g. haemophilia.

Let B = normal dominant blood clotting gene and h = recessive haemophilia gene.

parents: mother (XBXh)   x   Father (XBY-)
          (carrier)   (normal)

	XB	Xh
XB	XbXB	XBXh
Y-	XBY-	XhY-

sex cells: XB or Xh   XB or Y-

B and h alleles are on the X chromosome (sex linked) — that is why they move with these chromosomes during meiosis.

offspring: 1 XBXB   1 XBXh   1 XBY-   1 XhY-
            normal   carrier   normal   haemophiliac
            female   female   male   male

- Haemophiliac males tend not to have children because of the difficulties of having the disease.
- Usually only males develop haemophilia.
- Only males get one form of muscular dystrophy — it is passed on in the same way.
- Females can be colour blind even though it is inherited in the same way — colour blind males will want to have children as the condition is not life-threatening.

Let C = normal vision and c = colour blind
Mother (XCXc) – a carrier x father (XcY-) – colour blind.
There is a 25% chance of the genotype XcXc – a colour blind female.

Structure of DNA

- Two long strands that coil around each other to form a **double helix** shape.
- Strands are linked together by **hydrogen bonds** – from one base to another.
- There are 4 bases (chemicals) in DNA – called A, T, C, and G.
  DNA is able to replicate itself exactly:
- The double helix 'unzips' – each side acts as a template to build another DNA strand.
- Result is **two** double helixes of DNA.
- These are separated into new cells as the cell cytoplasm divides.
- Happens to all chromosomes (the strands of DNA) at the same time so the division of cells is co-ordinated.

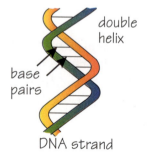

* = hydrogen bond

Protein synthesis

- Order of the bases of DNA is very important.
- These code for all proteins.
- Three nucleic acid bases code for one amino acid – called triplet code.

Examiner's tip
A hard topic – grade A questions – don't worry if you don't understand – you can still get a B or C without this!

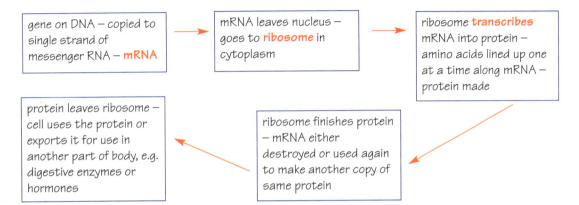

Mutation

- Change in the gene code – DNA instructions are changed – can happen anytime when DNA replicates.
- Gene mutations that occur when ova and sperm are being produced – passed on to the offspring – embryo will not survive gestation if the mutation is too great.
- Only small mutations are passed on in this way, e.g. Down's Syndrome – this is when one sex cell, usually an ovum, contains one extra chromosome – the embryo has 47 chromosomes instead of 46 in every cell – this affects development and produces the symptoms of a Down's Syndrome child.

Chromosome changes in adults

- Cells divide and produce new cells – the process of making new chromosomes can go wrong.
- Mutations can occur naturally with a mistake in replication of DNA – the mutation is usually fatal for the cell and it will die.
- The dead cell is destroyed by the immune system and no harm results.

Some mutations are caused by ionising radiation such as:

- Ultra violet – gamma rays – X-rays.
- Also caused by chemicals such as tar from cigarettes.
- Greater exposure – more mutations – greater chance that a cell can survive – cell will replicate and pass mutation on to daughter cells – this mutation remains in the one organism – unless mutation is where sex cells are made.
- Cancer – serious mutation – when cells lose their ability to stop dividing – cells grow out of control – lose contact inhibition – cells normally stop growing on contact.

VARIATION, INHERITANCE AND EVOLUTION

Cell division

Mitosis

Body cell division – repair and growth.

> Know the difference between **mitosis** and **meiosis**.

- Cells divide – produce copies of themselves – all their pairs of chromosomes are duplicated exactly.
- Two new cell nuclei receive identical sets of paired chromosomes.
- All body cells have identical chromosomes – there are occasional mistakes – which are **chromosome mutations**.

Meiosis

Production of sex cells.

> Look up some diagrams - a CD-ROM is good if your school has one - ask your teacher - so you know what happens in mitosis and meiosis.

- Copies of chromosomes made in the **testes of males** after puberty – in the **ovaries of females** before they are born – in **ovaries** and **anthers** of plants.
- Pairs of chromosomes separated.
- The cell divides to form four sex cells – each sex cell only has one copy of the chromosome.

Genetic engineering

- When genes are transferred from one living thing to another.
- Between members of the same or different species.

Benefits

Conquering cystic fibrosis.

> Be prepared to write a short essay to discuss advantages and disadvantages of genetic engineering.

- A healthy gene could be placed into a cell in an embryo.
- This would divide and provide the embryo with normal secretions in the lungs.
  or
- The same gene could be transferred via a virus directly into the lungs of a cystic child.
- The virus is genetically engineered to carry the healthy gene – it infects the lungs of the child – the healthy gene is transferred and starts to work in the child.

Producing human Factor 8.

- Human Factor 8 gene is inserted into DNA of bacterial cell.
- The bacteria can be cultured – it produces the human protein coded by the gene.
- Factor 8 is collected, purified and used by haemophiliacs (whose blood does not clot).

Disadvantages.

- How far do scientists go?
- Do we clone human beings?
- Do we select the genes of our children?
- The moral debate will continue.

Tissue culture

A small group of cells is taken from a plant or animal – then grown using special media and chemicals such as hormones.

Advantages

- You can produce thousands of identical plants from one small tissue culture.
- All of the plants are genetically identical – **clones**.
- Human or animal cells can also be grown in cultures – they don't form living things, just sheets of cells – these can be used to test drugs, etc. – this saves using live animals.
- **Embryo transplants** are carried out in this way – a fertilised ovum produces a ball of cells – this ball of cells can be split up and each cell goes on to develop into an embryo – vets can use this technique if a farmer wants to produce lots of identical offspring in cattle, pigs or sheep.

Cloning

This is not quite genetic engineering – not altering genes but manipulating cells or cell nuclei – techniques used in both plants and animals.

Problems

- Moral questions about human use of cultured embryos.
- Genes in the clones are all the same – can cause problems.
- There is a lack of variation – the evolutionary process has been stopped.
- Wild herds must be kept alive in order to maintain a large number of natural genes for future generations to breed from.

Selective breeding

- Humans use knowledge of genetics to select which animals and plants to breed.
- The right choice of animals to breed from could improve the herd.
- You could end up with herds of cows that produce more milk – pigs that grow bigger – disease-resistant cereals.

Two forms of reproduction

- **Sexual** – this mixes genes and produces much more variation in living things – evolution happens.
- **Asexual** – produces offspring that are identical – the offspring are clones – they are all genetically the same.

Evolution

Evidence comes from **fossils** which are found in rocks. Fossils show us how living things have changed – or stayed the same – over millions of years.

Other evidence from DNA testing etc.

Formation of fossils

- Hard parts of animals and plants do not decay easily – covered by sand/silt – replaced over millions of years by minerals in rocks – the animal/plant becomes a rock – fossil.
- Sometimes formed from soft tissues which did not decay – because the microbes that decay matter were absent or there was no oxygen to help the decay process.
- Life evolved over 3,000 million years ago.
- The living things today evolved from living things from the past – life evolved from the first simple living things.
- Evolution takes millions of years and many animals and plants have become extinct.
- The changes in living things are shown in the fossil record – evidence that supports the theory of evolution.

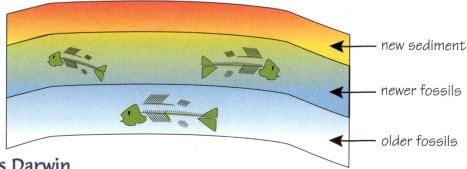

Charles Darwin

Over many years of study he made four observations that led to his theory of evolution by natural selection:

- All living things have the potential to over-produce offspring.
- Population numbers tend to remain constant over long periods of time.
- All living things show variation within their species.
- Some types of variation are inherited – genetic variation.

Natural selection

This is how evolution happens. One species of living thing has many individual differences and the differences are passed on in the parents' genes from generation to generation by reproduction. The process is as follows:

- One characteristic is very well suited to the environment.
- It may give the animal or plant and its offspring an advantage.
- The advantage, e.g. camouflage in an insect, means that the animal survives – passes on its genes to its offspring – this could lead to evolution.
- Over many generations the camouflage may get better and the species changes colour or shape.
- Thus the characteristics of an animal or plant that are suited to the environment are passed on from one generation to the next.
- The living things that 'fit' into their environment will survive, those that are less well adapted could become extinct.

Peppered moth - an example of natural selection

- Lichen grows on trees in unpolluted areas.
- Moth is naturally light coloured – camouflage against light lichen-covered bark on trees – better adapted.
- Dark varieties occur naturally by mutation – usually eaten by predators – no camouflage.
- Polluted areas – no lichen – blackened tree bark – dark moths camouflaged – better adapted – light moths eaten.
- Population changed in polluted areas to dark moths.
- Two populations evolved – light in clean areas – dark in polluted air areas.
- Pollution diminishing – dark moths becoming rare as tree bark covered in lichens again – light coloured moths increasing in numbers – they are better camouflaged – better adapted.

A dark variety of moth may have become a sub-species but cleaner air has reversed this line of evolution.

Questions

VARIATION, INHERITANCE AND EVOLUTION

1 How many chromosomes are in a human cell nucleus? _____

2 What do you call the 'packages' of information on chromosomes? _____

3 What chemical are chromosomes made from? _____

4 How many chromosomes are there in a human sperm cell? _____

5 Which four observations led to Darwin's theory of evolution? _____

_____

_____

6 Which is the chromosome pair for sex determination in a human male? _____

7 Which word describes species of living things which no longer exist? _____

Use the words below to describe the following pairs of genes for questions 8 to 12:

A. homozygous recessive   B. homozygous dominant   C. heterozygous
(If N = normal gene and is dominant, c = gene for cystic fibrosis and is recessive.)

8 The genotype cc. _____

9 The genotype Nc. _____

(If B = brown eyes and is dominant, b = blue eyes and is recessive.)

10 Bb. _____

11 BB. _____

12 bb. _____

13 What gives us the most information about evolution? _____

14 By what process does evolution occur? _____

15 How long ago did life evolve on earth? _____

16 What are genetically identical living things called? _____

17 What is the name of the process where farmers and vets control the breeding of animals? _____

18 What is the process of body cell division called? _____

19 What is the process of sex cell division called? _____

20 What do we call the process where genes are transferred from one living thing to another? _____

21 Which types of radiation cause mutations? _____

_____

Microbes, disease and biotechnology

Microbes

Fungi

These include organisms as large as toadstools and as microscopically small as yeast.

- Cells of fungi have a cell wall – DNA is inside a nucleus.
- Yeast – used in brewing and baking industry – can be grown on simple media like agar.
- Other fungi like the mould **penicillium** also need vitamins to grow.
- Fungi are vital to the world – are the major decomposers of dead material.
- Living things that decay dead material are called **saprophytes**.
- Diseases caused include – athlete's foot.

Protozoa

These single celled animals have a membrane, nucleus and cytoplasm – vary from a simple **Amoeba** to the complicated **Paramecium**.

- Protozoa feed on bacteria and dead and decaying matter.
- Can cause disease – e.g. **malaria**, diarrhoea – most are very useful to man because they decompose decayed matter.
- Used in sewage treatment.

Bacteria

These are much larger than viruses, with more complex structures and a lot more DNA.

- Contain cytoplasm – surrounded by a thin membrane – DNA not inside a nucleus.
- Some very hardy – will survive for years as spores – until conditions for growth are right, e.g. **anthrax**.
- Others cannot survive outside a living host.
- Can reproduce outside cells – when they cause disease they destroy cells and use the contents for food.
- Bacterial **metabolism** produces **toxins** (poisons) which can cause disease.
- Diseases caused by bacteria include TB, whooping cough, tetanus.
- Bacteria can be grown in culture (e.g. on agar plates) – culture contains food – soil bacteria may need only carbohydrate and minerals – disease causing bacteria (pathogens) may need blood or protein together with vitamins to grow in culture.
- All bacteria need water/moisture and some warmth to grow.
- Most bacteria are harmless to humans and are very beneficial.
- They decompose dead matter in the soil.
- In your intestine they help digest your food and make vitamins.
- They can be used to produce chemicals for our use, e.g. antibiotics, Factor 8 – genetic engineering.

Viruses

These are small particles made of protein and either DNA or RNA.

- Very few genes – gene for each protein – genes control replication of virus inside the cell it invades.
- RNA viruses thought to be very primitive – many have been around since the first chemicals of life appeared on Earth.
- The most dangerous virus yet found is an RNA virus called **ebola** which is a **filovirus**.
- Viruses need a living cell in order to replicate – some can survive as crystals outside a cell for a long time.
- Diseases caused by viruses are – **polio, AIDS, influenza, colds, chicken pox**.
- Viruses can be grown in cultures of **living cells**.

Louis Pasteur

- World-renowned French chemist and biologist.
- Founded the science of microbiology.
- Proved the germ theory of disease.
- Invented the process of pasteurisation.
- Developed vaccines for several diseases, including rabies.

Rabies vaccine

- After experimenting with the saliva of animals suffering from this disease, Pasteur concluded that the disease rests in the nerve centres of the body.
- An extract from the spinal column of a rabid dog was injected into the bodies of healthy animals – symptoms of rabies were produced.
- By studying the tissues of infected animals, particularly rabbits, Pasteur was able to develop an attenuated (changed and harmless) form of the virus that could be used for inoculation.
- In 1885, a young boy and his mother arrived at Pasteur's laboratory – the boy had been bitten badly by a rabid dog – Pasteur was urged to treat him with his new method – at the end of the treatment, which lasted ten days the boy was being inoculated with the most potent rabies virus known – he recovered and remained healthy – since that time, thousands of people have been saved from rabies by this treatment.

Pasteur's evidence

Pasteur carried out many simple experiments which showed that spontaneous generation did not occur, and he could produce infections when he wanted.

- Several flasks were produced with **sterile** growth media – prevents contamination.
- The flasks were different shapes as shown.
- Flasks 1 to 3 contained sterile culture media (sterilised by boiling) – flask 4 was not sterilised.

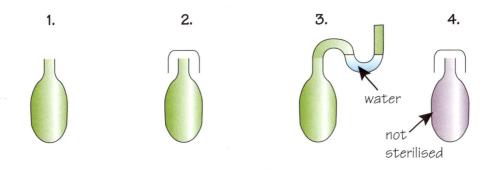

- Flask 1 was left open, became contaminated and culture media decomposed.
- Flask 2 was covered and remained sterile.
- Flask 3 remained sterile as the water trap prevented the entry of microbes.
- Flask 4 was contaminated and culture media decomposed.

Disease

Diseases may be caused by:

- **Microbes** that invade the body – called **pathogens**.
- Toxins from microbes – e.g. in food poisoning.
- Animals that invade the body – called **parasites**, e.g. malaria.
- Toxins from the environment, e.g. asbestosis of the lungs, lead poisoning.
- Poor diet – rickets – lack of calcium or vitamin D.
- Gene mutations – many types of cancer.
- Heredity – cystic fibrosis, etc.

Microbial disease

- Caused by **toxins** – poisons – produced by growing microbes.
- Growth of microbes in cells – cell death.
- Made much worse by person being weak – e.g. AIDS.
- Usually need a lot of microbes to cause disease – unhygienic conditions – e.g. food poisoning (bacteria) – or contact with infection – e.g. chicken pox (virus).

Malaria

- Caused by parasite called **Plasmodium**.
- Carried by several species of **mosquito – insect vector**.
- Mosquito injects parasite when sucking human blood.
- Parasite invades body cells – red blood cells and liver – feeds and reproduces.
- Cells die and produce symptoms of disease – fever, etc.
- Parasite returns to mosquito from human blood when mosquito feeds.
- Parasite changes form and reproduces in mosquito.
- Cycle starts over again.

New mosquitos and people are infected to perpetuate the disease.

Food poisoning/spoilage

- Microbes can contaminate food.
- Grow and produce toxins – cause food poisoning and spoil food.

Preserving food

You may need to discuss this in the form of a short essay.

- Ultra high heat – kills microbes, e.g. UHT milk.
- Pasteurisation – destroys dangerous germs but not lactobacilli – milk can still go sour.
- Drying – removes water – microbes cannot grow.
- Freezing – does not kill microbes – stops growth – water not available – when re-hydrated food can become contaminated and decay.
- Salt and sugar – dissolved in water – can preserve food by osmosis – water not available to microbes – used to dissolve solute.
- Canning – foods can be heated – also use salt/sugar – osmosis again.
- Irradiation – gamma rays destroy microbes – food unaffected – some scientists believe vitamin content of irradiated foods is affected – research continues.
- Chemical preservatives.

Microbial diseases are usually **infectious** while other diseases are usually **non-infectious**.

Defence

- **Skin** – is a barrier to microbes.
- **Blood clot** – wounds are easily sealed – prevents entry of microbes.
- **Mucus** – sticky to trap microbes – protects nose, mouth – then lungs and stomach – open to outside – stomach has acid – kills most microbes.
- **Antibiotics** – chemicals usually produced by microbes to kill other microbes, e.g. penicillin – produced by a fungus to kill bacteria.
- Antibiotics **do not kill viruses only bacteria and fungi** – new antibiotics are needed all the time – resistant microbes evolve due to over-use of antibiotics.
- **Immune system** – white blood cells – antibodies – see blood – circulation.
- **Immunisation** – using vaccines to prepare the immune system to fight an infection – produces antibodies – vaccines are produced from a less dangerous form or dead form of bacteria or viruses – can also be prepared from proteins and toxins.

Note some microbes are difficult to vaccinate against, e.g. common cold – virus mutates regularly and changes protein coat – a new virus is not recognised – you get another cold – every cold you have had was caused by a different virus.

Vaccines

Be prepared to discuss the advantages and disadvantages of vaccination.

There are five ways of producing vaccines.

- Using a killed virulent (can easily cause disease) organism, e.g. whooping cough or polio vaccine (Sweden).
- Using a live but non-virulent strain of the microbe – can be produced by genetic engineering or selective culturing, e.g. TB, polio (GB), rubella.
- Chemically altering a toxin molecule – still has the shape of the toxin – still an antigen – but no longer dangerous, e.g. diphtheria, tetanus.

- Separating the surface antigens from the microbe – these are usually protein molecules – the antigens can be used as the vaccine, e.g. influenza.
- Use genetically engineered bacteria to produce the viral antigen, e.g. hepatitis B – the antigen is the vaccine – no virus is injected.

Vaccination has helped to make the world a healthier place – some diseases have been wiped out, e.g. smallpox – some people react against the vaccine – very few – they may be severely brain-damaged as a result.

Hygiene

Can prevent the spread of many diseases.

- Coughing and sneezing spread the cold virus – use a handkerchief.
- Sharing towels/wearing other people's shoes – spreads athlete's foot.
- Antiseptics – kill microbes on living tissues.
- Disinfectants – kill microbes anywhere.
- Living conditions and lifestyle can cause or prevent the spread of disease.
- Precautions when handling, storing and cooking food.

Biotechnology and mankind

Medicine

Many areas of medicine use modern biotechnology:

- Modern materials for joint replacement.
- Heart pacemakers, valves and transplants.
- Kidney machines and transplants.
- Antibiotics and vaccines – some produced by genetic engineering.

Transplants

Donors are needed – tissue rejection is a problem.

To prevent rejection:

- Donor and patient 'tissue type' is matched.
- Bones may be irradiated to inhibit the production of white cells – reduced immune response.
- Patient kept in sterile conditions – susceptible to infections – immune response knocked out.
- Use immuno-suppressive drugs – leaves patient prone to infections – this treatment may last a long time.

Food

Yoghurt

- Starting product is milk.
- Starter culture of bacteria is added to warm milk (30ºC).
- Culture ferments the milk sugar called lactose and produces lactic acid.
- Lactic acid causes the protein in milk to thicken.
- Different types of bacteria cause slightly different end results – the bacteria are all called **lactobacilli**.

Cheese

- Bacteria are allowed to turn the milk into a solid mass.
- Different bacteria produce different flavours.
- Can add new microbes at this point to improve the flavour, e.g. penicillium when making blue stilton, etc.

Brewing

- Yeast – respires anaerobically (without oxygen).
- Produces alcohol and carbon dioxide.
- Beers and wines are produced.

Baking

- Sugar and yeast are mixed with bread dough.
- Yeast ferments the sugar and produces carbon dioxide – makes bread rise.
- Happens when the dough is left in a warm place.
- Alcohol is also produced – this evaporates during baking.

Baby food

- Enzymes called proteases are used to pre-digest protein in some baby foods.
- Makes it easier for babies' digestive systems to digest the meal.

Soft centre chocolates

- Starch is not sweet and is solid.
- It is flavoured in the centre of a chocolate.
- Enzyme amylase (a carbohydrase) is added to the starch.
- Starch is converted into glucose.
- Chocolate centre becomes sweet and liquid.

Slimming aids

- Glucose is the main sugar used in foods.
- Also the most abundant sugar produced by plants during photosynthesis.
- Glucose can be converted into **fructose** by an enzyme called **isomerase**.
- Fructose tastes much sweeter than glucose – less can be used to sweeten food.
- Less 'sugar' means less energy (kilo joules or calories) – so slimming foods can taste just as sweet but have less calories.
- Slimming foods are more expensive because of the need to produce **fructose** using enzymes.

Fermenters

Most fermenters have the following features:

- A water-cooled jacket to remove excess heat from the fermentation process – temperature of the fermenter is important as microbes need to be kept at the **optimum temperature** for their enzymes to function.
- A stirrer – automated to keep all the microbes in contact with the food supplied.
- An air supply which may be necessary for respiration. (Remember that some microbes are **anaerobic** or produce useful products under anaerobic conditions – in such cases oxygen would be **excluded** from the process.)
- Sensors for measuring temperature, pH, oxygen, nutrient content (e.g. glucose electrode) and product concentrations.
- Supply of substrate – the food material for the microbe.

Fermentation

- Fuels based on ethanol (alcohol) can be produced by fermenting waste materials.
- Sugar cane juice or glucose produced by adding enzymes to maize starch – used as raw materials for fermenting sugar into alcohol.
- Alcohol can be used as fuel for vehicles.

In the developing world, where energy resources are scarce, we can grow plant material and use the products to produce gas or alcohol as a fuel source for the home and transport. This is a renewable resource as the plant material can be grown every year.

Antibiotics – penicillin

- Discovered by **Alexander Fleming** – accidentally found that a mould which had contaminated a culture dish was destroying bacteria in the culture.
- He cultured the mould and repeated the experiments – the mould destroyed many different bacteria.
- **Florey and Chain** isolated the active agent from penicillin and developed its use as an antibiotic.

Manufacture of penicillin

- Fermenter is used.
- This is filled with culture medium – contains all food that mould needs to grow.
- Starter culture of **Penicillium** is used – added to the culture medium.
- During first 24 hours the cells multiply quickly.
- When they start to run short of energy, i.e. sugar – they start to produce penicillin.
- After about 7 days penicillin concentration is at its maximum.
- Culture is filtered – penicillin extracted from the filtrate.

Biogas

- Mainly the gas methane.
- Microbes produce methane in large quantities as a result of anaerobic respiration.
- Food source of anaerobic respiration is sugar or carbohydrate – in fermentation is usually glucose or another sugar.
- Biogas generator can be used on a small scale – individual farms or villages – waste products can be used as energy source for microbes.

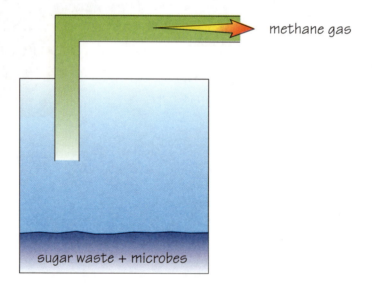

For example, villages in India have small biogas generators that use cattle dung. Villagers collect the dung and fill the generator. The microbes decompose the dung and produce methane as a waste product. The methane is piped to village houses and used for cooking.

- Biogas can also be used on a larger scale.
- Waste from sewage farms or sugar factories used to produce methane gas.
- Food factories like sugar refineries or breweries have waste products that contain a lot of sugar.

- Waste is fed into a large scale biogas generator.
- Microbes are added in a culture.
- Microbes ferment the sugar and produce methane gas.
- Methane is used to supply factory with heat – even to provide energy for the manufacturing process.
- Burning methane can turn water into steam – will turn a generator – produces electricity.

Batch culture

- Microbes and the substrate are fermented in a container – can be large or small.
- Allowed to finish fermentation.
- Usually takes about 10 days.
- This is how beer and wine are brewed.

Continuous culture

- Culture is allowed to feed continually on a substrate (e.g. sugar).
- Substrate is constantly supplied over a period of weeks.
- Liquid from the culture is constantly drawn off and the product removed.
- Amount of product is greater than from a normal batch culture.
- Industry uses continuous culture where possible – more profit from the process.
- Antibiotics are produced in this manner as well as Factor 8 – blood clotting protein needed by haemophiliacs.

Enzymes

Enzymes can be extracted from cells and microbes after they have been cultured. Science can make microbes produce any enzyme by the process of **genetic engineering**. Enzyme technology is a fast growing and advancing science.

In the home we use biological washing powders:

- Biological detergents contain two types of enzyme.
- Proteases digest protein to soluble amino acids.
- Lipases digest fats to soluble fatty acids and glycerol.
- Enzymes are temperature sensitive and most are denatured by high temperatures – therefore biological detergents are usually low temperature agents.
- There are bacteria that live in hot springs whose enzymes work at high temperatures.
- These enzymes may form the basis, after genetic engineering, of better biological agents that even work at 90°C.
- Enzymes are proteins that control chemical reactions – work on a simple 'lock and key' theory.
- Enzyme has a shape – like all proteins.
- Shape fits the 'lock' of the substrate – enzyme has an active site or sites.
- Chemical reaction takes place – substrate changes – products released.
- Enzyme free to react with another substrate molecule.

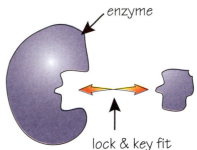

Enzymes are affected by temperature and pH:

- Temperature – only at optimum temperature is enzyme perfect shape – key fit for lock.
- Low temperature – shape altered – enzyme does not fit properly – active site shape altered – reaction slowed – enzyme is **not** destroyed.
- Warm a cold enzyme – changes shape back to optimum.
- High temperature – enzyme changes shape – if too high enzyme **denatures**.
- Enzyme destroyed – active sites no longer exist.
- Cool enzyme – function does **not** return – enzyme completely denatured.
- pH – enzyme has optimum pH as well.
- Change pH – change enzyme active sites – enzyme may be denatured.

Enzyme technology

- Enzymes control chemical reactions.
- Industrial processes can use enzymes to speed up chemical reactions or allow processes to occur at much lower temperatures and pressures – saves energy and money for the company.
- If whole microbes used as source of enzymes – have to be kept alive for long periods.
- One advantage of this is that continuous culture can be used instead of batch culture.

Enzyme alginates

- Some enzymes can be purified from their living systems.
- Enzymes are proteins – such large molecules can be attached to alginate beads.
- Beads can be packed into columns.
- Substrate trickled down the column.
- Product comes out of the bottom of the column.

  This process could be something as simple as the following:
- Glucose solution as the substrate.
- Enzyme isomerase on alginate beads.
- Trickle the substrate down column and over alginate beads.
- Solution leaving the bottom of the column will be fructose – used in slimming aids.

  Using enzymes in this way is called immobilisation.

  Immobilising enzymes has several advantages over using live microbes:
- Don't need to keep the microbes alive, which makes the process easier to run.
- Enzymes are easily stored and transported if necessary – means that small scale processes can be portable.
- Enzymes can easily be recovered from the substrate and re-used if some lost from the alginate beads.
- Most inert substances, e.g. alginate, hold the enzymes securely so that very little enzyme is lost in the process.

Food production - SCP - single cell protein - made from single cell organisms.

Bacteria, yeast, other fungi and single-celled algae can be grown quickly and economically in both batch culture and continuous culture. These organisms are a valuable source of protein:

- Protein can be used as a food supplement or processed into food itself, e.g. **quorn**.
- Quorn is made from mycoprotein – protein extracted from the mycelia of growing fungi.
- Bacterial and algal protein can be used in the same way.

Questions

1 What is a saprophyte? _____

2 What type of microbe causes malaria? _____

3 Which vaccine did Pasteur develop? _____

4 What is a pathogen?_____

5 Which animal transmits malaria?_____

6 Name 5 ways of preserving food. _____

7 What is an antibiotic? _____

8 What is meant by immunisation? _____

9 Name 5 ways of producing vaccines. _____

_____

_____

_____

10 What is an antiseptic? _____

11 What is a disinfectant? _____

12 How does biotechnology help people with:

(a) heart problems _____

(b) kidney failure _____

(c) arthritis of the hip? _____

13 What process is used to manufacture penicillin?_____
_____

14 How is biogas produced? _____
_____

15 What is batch culture? _____
_____

16 What is continuous culture?_____
_____

17 How are enzymes used in the home?_____
_____

18 What is SCP? _____
_____

MICROBES, DISEASE AND BIOTECHNOLOGY

Living things and their environment

Adaptation and competition

The following affect all living things:

- **Temperature** – affects the rate at which enzymes work in all cells – plant and animal – animals and plants may be adapted to withstand very high or low temperatures.

- **Light** – affects photosynthesis – most plants lose their leaves in winter – not enough light for photosynthesis – also too cold for enzymes to work – most animals need light to hunt and find food – some animals are nocturnal which means they come out at night and sleep during the day.

- **Water** – needed by all living things – if there is little water there is little life – animals and plants can be specialised, e.g. desert animals and plants. Note – if the ground freezes plants cannot obtain water through their roots, the same as in the desert.

- **Oxygen** – needed for aerobic respiration – not usually a problem on land but can be a problem in water – oxygen levels may fall as result of sewage or natural decay in the river or lake.

- **Carbon dioxide** – needed for photosynthesis in plants.

  The above factors can change during 24 hours. Animals may be adapted to feed at certain times of the day. Plants may open leaves or flowers only at certain times of the day.

- **Space** – all living things need space to live – an area to find food – or enough light for photosynthesis.

  All the above factors can be reasons why different plants live in different areas. They also explain why animals live in different places and even move around during one day or a whole year.

  Living things live where the conditions suit them. They are in competition with each other.

Population size

In a **community** of animals and plants living in a certain **habitat**, the size of a population of any living thing may be affected by **competition** for/with:

- **Food** – animals and plants compete for food resources – those that are successful will survive to breed.
- **Space and light** – plants – photosynthesis needs light – animals – carnivore needs a certain area to live in – must be enough prey animals for food – will often defend this area as its territory and drive away any other predators.
- **Living things** – herbivores restrict the growth and population of plants – carnivores restrict the population of herbivores and other creatures.

- **Man** – can remove or introduce species – this has effect on the whole food chain – the effect may be devastating, e.g. grey squirrel vs. red squirrel.
- **Disease** – may deplete a population – e.g. myxomatosis kills rabbits.

Human impact on the environment

> **Examiner's tip**
> This may be in your physics exam — fossil fuels — power stations.

Air pollution

- **Sulphur dioxide** and **nitrogen oxides**.
- Produced when fossil fuels are burnt in furnaces and engines.
- These gases are dangerous – can cause asthma attacks in cities.
- Gases dissolve in rain water to produce acid rain.
- This can kill plants – if the acid content of rivers and lakes becomes too high, animals and plants cannot survive.

Increasing human population

- Raw materials – resources of the Earth are being rapidly used up.
- Many of them are non-renewable.
- The greater the standard of living of the population, the faster resources are used.
- This leads to more waste which could lead to greater pollution unless there are adequate controls.

The management of the Earth's resources and the waste produced by mankind is one of the biggest problems to be solved in the twenty-first century.

Water pollution

Polluted water can interfere with all of life's processes.

Pollutants

- **Factory waste** – may include acid, cyanide or metals such as mercury and lead.
- **Acid irritates cells** – damages plant roots – fish gills – kills fish.
- **Cyanide** is a poison of the respiratory system and prevents cells from releasing energy – cyanide can kill in seconds – enters food chain.
- **Mercury and lead** affect bone and nerve cells.

Fertilisers

- Sprayed onto fields for increased crop production.
- Minerals are soluble – get washed away into rivers and lakes.
- Fertilisers increase the growth of algae in water.
- Water can turn green with algae in a badly affected lake.
- Algae absorb the light and stop it from reaching plants under the surface.
- Bottom-living plants die.

LIVING THINGS AND THEIR ENVIRONMENT

49

- Dead plants are decomposed by bacteria using oxygen from the water.
- Water becomes depleted in oxygen – animals suffocate.
- Bottom-living plants also hold the mud with their roots – when they die a lot of mud and silt may be washed down to the sea.
- River banks may collapse.
- Ecosystem of a river or lake may be damaged.

Water becoming deoxygenated by decomposition of dead matter is called **eutrophication**. Polluting water with untreated sewage has the same effect.

Deforestation

- Plants absorb carbon dioxide during photosynthesis.
- Release carbon dioxide during respiration – absorbing more than they give out.
- If large numbers are destroyed then the level of CO_2 in the air will increase.
- Wood is often burnt – releases more carbon dioxide.
- Tropical rainforests contain an enormous number of plants and they are being destroyed at an alarming rate.
- Could mean more carbon dioxide remains in the atmosphere.
- More heat would be trapped – increase in temperature – increased **greenhouse effect**.

The greenhouse effect

- The Earth is warm – has an insulating layer of air – this traps some of the heat from the Sun and prevents it from being re-radiated back into space – **greenhouse effect**.
- Water and carbon dioxide absorb heat and radiate it back to the Earth's surface.
- This enables life on Earth to survive – recently has been giving cause for concern.
- Atmosphere has 0.03% of carbon dioxide – this level of carbon dioxide has been increasing over recent years – increased burning of fossil fuels – destruction of the tropical rainforests.
- Estimated that a doubling of CO_2 levels will mean a rise in temperature of 2°C.
- Other gases that trap heat include methane, some chlorofluorocarbons and nitrous oxides.
- Methane is produced in the intestines of cattle – it is also produced by rice plants as they grow – as we produce more rice and beef or milk we are increasing levels of methane in the atmosphere – adding to the greenhouse effect.

Weigh up the evidence and form your own opinions - be prepared to discuss it!

Increasing temperature may mean:

- Changes in weather.
- Therefore problems with food production.
- A rise in sea level.
- Therefore problems in some coastal areas for all living things – loss of environment.

Be prepared to write a short essay on this!

Energy and nutrient transfer

Sun is source of energy for all life on Earth.

Producers

- Green plants – they capture the energy from the Sun.
- Store this energy in their cells.
- Some energy used – growth and repair, making protein, fat, etc.
- Some is lost as waste, e.g. heat.

Consumers

- Animals – some eat plants – energy of the plant is taken in.
- Energy used for repair, growth, making proteins, e.g. hormones, enzymes.
- Respiration produces energy for the living processes.
- Energy is lost in faeces – also as waste from chemical reactions in cells.
- Energy is lost as heat – animals move and produce heat – heat energy is lost to the air.
- Mammals and birds lose more energy this way – warm blooded – homoiothermic.

Decomposers

- Microbes – bacteria and fungi.
- Dead materials are completely decomposed – all the energy originally captured by the plant finds its way back into the environment.

Pollution enters the food chain, e.g.

- Mercury builds up in plant tissue.
- Fish that eat plants get mercury in their diet.
- Mercury level builds up in fish – may kill the fish.
- Fish eaten by predator such as an otter or pike.
- These tertiary consumers get high doses of mercury in their diet – will eventually kill them.

It is often the tertiary consumer that is killed by pollution. The levels of poison may not be high enough in the producer or primary consumer, but the level increases the further along the food chain you go, often reaching lethal levels at the final predator.

plant → fish → otter (poisoned by mercury)
mercury

LIVING THINGS AND THEIR ENVIRONMENT

Food chains

These link all living things together – each stage of a food chain is called a 'trophic level'.

E.g. a mouse eats some grass. The mouse is eaten by an owl. This is the food chain:

- The arrow shows the direction that energy is moving.
- All food chains start with a green plant.
- All food chains end with an animal – usually a predator.

Food chains can be linked together to give a **food web**.
E.g. grass is also eaten by insects and voles. Shrews eat insects. Owls eat shrews and voles.

> **Examiner's tip**
> Be prepared to analyse and comment upon a food web that you haven't seen before!

> Think of arrow meaning 'eaten by'.

Food web

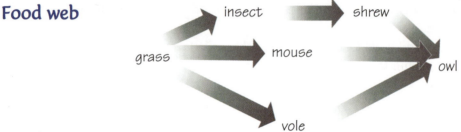

Food pyramids

This is a way of showing how many living things there are in a food chain or how much mass there is in a food chain.

E.g. food chain – grass ⟶ mouse ⟶ owl.

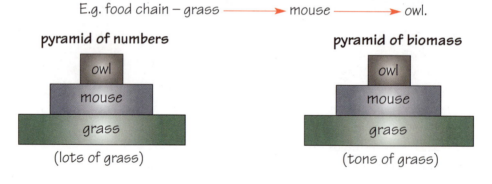

E.g. food chain – tree ⟶ insect ⟶ robin

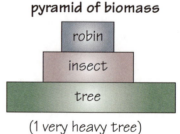

> A large tree has a strange number pyramid – there is only one living thing at the base – not millions.

Food chains lose energy between each trophic level – most food chains are short.
The shorter the food chain the more efficient the system.

Use of ecosystems

- Organisms are used by man for food – crops grown – animals kept on farms and fish caught in the sea.
- Efficient use of land – some areas unsuitable for crops – e.g. sheep raised on moorland which is unsuitable for crops.
- Crop yields increased by close planting – consider competition for light and water.
- Stocks of wild animals used for food by man can be depleted, e.g. fishing – need to control how many and what size of fish are caught.
- No control – fish population may crash and a valuable food source is lost for many years.

Careful management of natural stocks is needed and this may be achieved by governments co-operating to:

- Agree quotas for limits on how many animals are removed from the wild each year.
- Be selective in which animals are taken, e.g. only take non-breeding adult animals and not young or breeding animals.
- Avoid the animals' breeding season and not use breeding areas for fishing or hunting.

> Be prepared to write a short essay on managing food production.

Artifical ecosystems

Those created by humans – the amount of food produced in these areas is kept very high by:

- Using fertilisers.
- Using pesticides and fungicides to destroy pests.
- Reducing competition with wild animals and plants by various means.
- Bringing extra water by irrigation channels from reservoirs.
- Selectively breeding better animals and plants that are disease-resistant or grow bigger or faster.
- Using genetic engineering to produce disease-resistant crops.

This can have a major effect on natural ecosystems. The natural world needs consideration before man creates farmland. All domestic animals must be treated in a humane way while they are growing, being transported and eventually when they are killed.

Efficient artifical ecosystems

- Use short food chains – the shorter the food chain the less energy is lost between the links in the chain.
- Food animals lose energy when moved around – if man restricts the movement of animals they will grow faster – this is the reason behind factory farming – is it humane? – is it necessary?
- These animals are fed on plants – the plants need space to grow – so factory-farmed animals still need space for their food plants to grow.
- Control temperature – heat areas to reduce heat loss by animals.

LIVING THINGS AND THEIR ENVIRONMENT

The carbon cycle

- Carbon occurs in carbohydrate, protein and fat.
- Plants get their carbon from the air – carbon dioxide.
- Use it to make food by photosynthesis – build proteins, fats and carbohydrates.
- Animals get their carbon by eating plants and other animals.
- Respiration uses food – releases carbon dioxide back into the air.
- So plants **take in** carbon dioxide and living things **give out** carbon dioxide.
- Plants and animals die – bodies decompose – carbon in bodies enters environment.
- Dead matter is broken down by bacteria and other micro-organisms – decomposers.
- Decomposers also respire – carbon dioxide into the air.
- Burning – releases carbon dioxide into the air – extra carbon dioxide.

The exam question may not look like your N or C cycle. Don't worry - they are all the same. Learn the order of things, not just the pattern on the diagram. Revise by drawing your own flow charts.

The nitrogen cycle

- Nitrogen is needed to make proteins.
- Proteins build animal and plant tissue.
- Plants build proteins during photosynthesis – take nitrate out of the soil through roots.
- Animals eat plants – break down plant protein – build up animal protein.
- Animals excrete urea and faeces – contains nitrogen waste.
- Animals and plants die – the nitrogen can be returned to the cycle.
- Decomposing bacteria break the protein/urea/faeces down into ammonia (nitrogen + hydrogen).
- **Nitrifying bacteria** change this ammonia to nitrate (nitrogen + oxygen).
- Plant roots absorb nitrate – cycle begins again.

    Extras!
- **Denitrifying bacteria** change nitrate into nitrogen gas.
- **Nitrogen fixing bacteria** – take nitrogen out of the air and build it up into nitrates – can be found by themselves in the soil or living in the roots of plants belonging to the pea and bean family, e.g. clover, peas, etc. – these plants are called legumes.

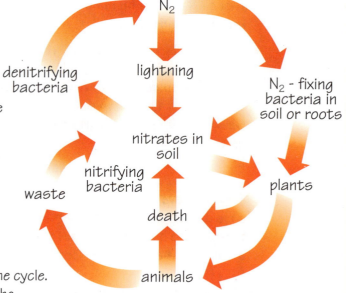

Classification of living things

The binomial system is used – each living thing has 2 names, e.g. man = Homo sapiens.

Living things are classified as:

- **Viruses.**
- **Bacteria.**
- **Protoctists** (protozoa).
- **Fungi** – see microbes/biotechnology.
- **Animals.**
- **Plants** – see below.

Animals are divided into **vertebrates** and **invertebrates**.

Invertebrates

Do not have a backbone – the different groups are:

- **Coelenterates** – have stinging cells – primitive soft bodies, e.g. jellyfish, anemone.
- **Flatworms** – e.g. tapeworm.
- **Annelid worms** – first group of animals to have segmented bodies – animals breathe through skin – restricts size of animal – not a large surface area for gaseous exchange – therefore animals do not grow particularly large, e.g. earthworm, leech.
- **Molluscs** – a large group – have many different forms – all have soft bodies – most have a shell, e.g. snail, mussel, limpet (have shells), slug, octopus (no shell), cuttlefish, squid (small shell inside body).
- **Echinoderms** – e.g. starfish, sea urchin.
- **Arthropods.**

Arthropods

These all have an external skeleton of hard material – exoskeleton.
They have jointed limbs and most have antennae. There are four groups:

- **Crustaceans** – most live in sea – many legs, two pairs of antennae, e.g. crabs, lobsters, prawns and woodlice (a crustacean!).
- Experiment – woodlice move towards dark and damp conditions – response to stimuli.
- **Insects** – six legs, wings, three body parts, one pair of antennae, compound eyes, e.g. flies, bees, beetles, etc.
- Complete metamorphosis – many insects show this, e.g. blowfly larvae (maggots) – feed on different food from adult – therefore animal can exploit different environments during its life cycle.
- Pollination – many plants pollinated by insects – very important to life on Earth.
- Bees specially adapted – collect pollen for hives – nectar for honey – important for fruit growers.
- **Arachnids** – eight legs, two body parts, many simple eyes, e.g. spiders, scorpions.
- **Myriapods** – many legs and body segments, e.g. millipedes and centipedes.

LIVING THINGS AND THEIR ENVIRONMENT

Vertebrates

Do have a backbone – the following groups are cold blooded (poikilothermic) – they don't produce heat inside their bodies:

- **Fish** – streamlined, live in water, tail for locomotion, breathe using gills, lay soft eggs in water, scaly skin, e.g. cod, pike, whale shark.
- **Gills** need to be very efficient – not as much oxygen in water as in air – have very large surface area – gills folded – many microscopic sections – water keeps gill filaments apart – supports them – good blood supply – in most fish blood flows opposite direction to water – counter-current flow – more efficient at gaseous exchange – fish out of water – suffocates – because large surface area disappears – no water to support filaments – all stick together – little surface available – fish dies.

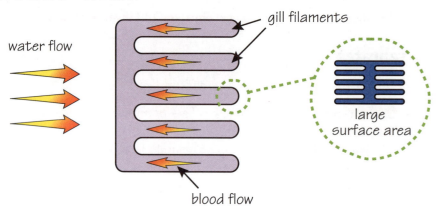

- **Amphibians** – live on land and in water, smooth slimy skin, breathe through skin, have lungs, use gills when tadpoles – lay soft eggs in water, e.g. newt, frog, toad and salamander – also show complete metamorphosis.
- **Reptiles** – have dry scaly skin, breathe air using lungs, lay soft shelled eggs on land, e.g. snakes, lizards, alligators, crocodiles.

The following groups are warm blooded (homoiothermic) – produce heat inside their bodies.

- **Birds** – have feathers, beaks and wings – most fly – lay hard shelled eggs on land, e.g. penguin, ostrich, finch, eagle, etc.
- **Mammals** – have fur or hair, feed young on milk from mammary glands, most produce young that develop inside the female's body, e.g. humans, cow, dog, whale, dolphin, duck-billed platypus (very primitive – lays eggs), kangaroo (marsupial mammal – young born immature and develop inside a pouch).

Plants

Have chlorophyll – two types – seed producers and those which do not produce seeds.

Seedless

- **Algae** – can be microscopic – primitive green plants – live in water – produce 80% of the Earth's oxygen as there are so many of them on the surface of the oceans, e.g. spirogyra, seaweed.
- **Mosses and liverworts** – no true roots, stems or leaves – no xylem or phloem – small, live on land – reproduce with spores, e.g. bog moss.
- **Ferns** – have roots, stems and leaves – young leaves coiled up in bud – reproduce using spores, e.g. horsetails, bracken.

Seed producers

- **Gymnosperms – conifers** – reproduce using cones – no true flowers but cones have seeds, e.g. larch, pine, etc.
- **Angiosperms** – flowering plants – have flowers and produce seeds inside a fruit, e.g. rose, oak, buttercup, etc.

Viruses

Only survive inside living cells – scientists still argue if they are truly alive – very small, e.g. cold, HIV, flu are caused by viruses.

Bacteria

Microscopic – most can live on their own – most are very useful, only a minority cause disease, e.g. streptococci (sore throats), tetanus, TB.

Fungi

Most are microscopic – they are **not** plants – no chlorophyll – most are decomposers in the soil – very useful, e.g. mushroom, toadstool, yeast – a few cause disease, e.g. some species of yeast.

Protoctists

Microscopic – most live in water – have all cell features – animal or plant, e.g. Amoeba, Paramecium (cells animal-like), Euglena (cells plant-like).

Questions

1 What is contained in fertiliser that is a serious pollutant of rivers?
_____

2 Why do living things need carbon? _____

3 Why do living things need nitrogen? _____

4 What is most plants' source of nitrogen? _____

5 What is a herbivore's source of nitrogen for amino acids? _____

6 What is a carnivore's source of nitrogen? _____

7 What is the name of the microbes that change nitrate into nitrogen gas?
_____

8 What is the name of the microbes that change nitrogen gas into nitrate?
_____

9 What is the end product of urine breakdown by nitrifying bacteria? _____

10 Which raw materials are used by plants to make amino acids during photosynthesis?
_____

11 What are the body features of insects? _____

12 Why do fish suffocate out of water? _____
_____

13 What is the waste product of plant respiration? _____

14 What is the waste product of animal respiration? _____

15 What % of the air is carbon dioxide? _____

16 Which type of microbe lives in the root nodules of legumes? _____

17 Which gas is mainly responsible for destructive 'acid rain'? _____

18 Which gases are responsible for the 'greenhouse effect'? _____
_____

19 Rain is often naturally slightly acid. Which gas is responsible for 'natural' acid rain?
_____

20 Which gases are the major pollutants from coal-fired power stations?
_____

21 Which pollutant will damage the gills of fish? _____

22 Which poison prevents cells from releasing energy? _____

Green plants as organisms

Structure of plants

Flowering plants have:

- **Roots** which anchor them to the ground.
- **Stems** to transport water and minerals to the leaves and flowers – the stem also transports food from the leaves to the roots.
- **Leaves** which use light, carbon dioxide and water to make food by *photosynthesis*.
- **Flowers** are the reproductive organs.

Photosynthesis

Plants **make food** by **photosynthesis**.

You must learn this equation!

$$\text{Carbon dioxide} + \text{water} \xrightarrow[\text{chlorophyll}]{\text{light}} \text{glucose} + \text{oxygen}$$

$$6CO_2 + 6H_2O \longrightarrow C_6H_{12}O_6 + 6O_2$$

Look up the experiments on photosynthesis! Remember you test leaves for starch using iodine. You need methylated spirit to remove the green colour from the leaf first!

- Photosynthesis is controlled by **enzymes**.
- All enzyme reaction rates are variable depending on the conditions.

Carbon dioxide

- Increase carbon dioxide = increased photosynthesis – only up to the point where the enzymes are working as fast as they can.
- Increase in carbon dioxide after this has little effect.
- Limited light will stop an increase in carbon dioxide from having any effect.

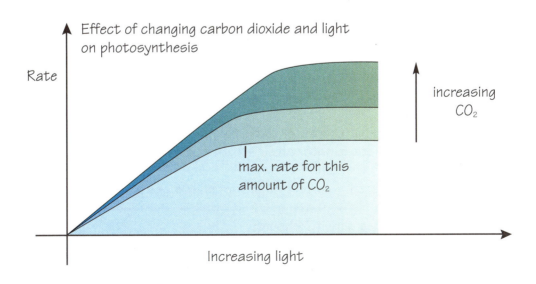

Light

- Increased light – increased photosynthesis – until the enzymes are working as fast as they can.
- Increasing light after this has little effect.
- Carbon dioxide – limited – will stop an increase in light from having any effect.
- Low temperature slows photosynthesis.
- Light absorbed by **chlorophyll** in **chloroplast**. Not all plant cells have chloroplasts – e.g. **epidermal** cells don't have chloroplasts – have a different function – protect the plant – specialised cells in the leaf called **palisade mesophyll** cells are specially adapted for photosynthesis.

Temperature

- Increased temperature – rate of photosynthesis increases up to the **optimum temperature** for the enzyme.
- Optimum temperature – enzyme shape is a perfect fit (lock and key idea).
- Above this temperature – enzyme shape starts to change – no longer fits perfectly – rate of reaction decreases – enzyme denatures at high temperature.
- Optimum temperature for photosynthesis depends on which environment the plant is adapted to, e.g. desert plants experience higher temperatures than British plants.

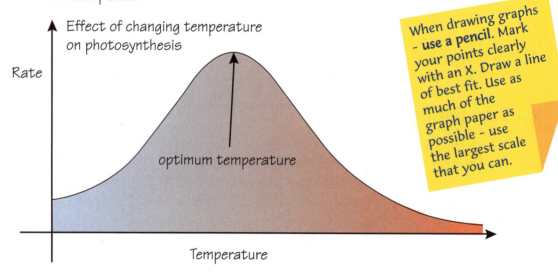

When drawing graphs - **use a pencil**. Mark your points clearly with an X. Draw a line of best fit. Use as much of the graph paper as possible - use the largest scale that you can.

Comparing photosynthesis and respiration

- Use hydrogen-carbonate indicator.
- Becomes redder with oxygen – usually very little CO_2 – yellow with carbon dioxide.
- Water plants turn indicator red – oxygen produced and carbon dioxide used.
- Water animals, e.g. water snails – turn indicator yellow – produce carbon dioxide – using oxygen.
- Balanced system – correct number of plants and animals – indicator orange.

Colour changes during 24 hours:
- Light = photosynthesis, indicator colour orange – red.
- Dark – no photosynthesis – indicator colour yellow – carbon dioxide produced by animals and plants.

Photosynthesis and growth

- Photosynthesis produces glucose then starch.
- Glucose/starch are made from carbon dioxide and water.
- Plants contain many other chemicals – proteins, amino acids, fats, fatty acids, glycerol, and DNA.
- Plants synthesise all these chemicals with the products of photosynthesis, using enzymes.
- To make the essential chemicals of life plants need to absorb minerals such as nitrate through their roots.
- Different minerals have different functions in the plant – see minerals.
- Photosynthesis produces oxygen – used by plants for respiration – excess released into atmosphere.

Growth occurs in:
- Root and shoot tips.
- Developing buds, flowers and fruits.
- Food storage organs – bulbs, tubers, etc.

Photosynthesis and assimilation

Assimilation means 'how food is used'. In plants the sugars produced by photosynthesis are used to:
- Produce starch which is stored as a future energy/raw material store.
- Converted to cellulose to make cell walls.
- With the addition of nitrogen and sometimes phosphorous and sulphur, converted into protein – proteins are used for growth – glucose is used to produce energy needed for growth.

Plants store carbohydrate as starch and not as sugars like glucose. This is because:
- Starch is insoluble.
- Therefore it does not cause large amounts of water to be stored in cells.
- Water enters cells by osmosis – see later section.

Transport of minerals and food

- Glucose and other nutrients are transported by phloem cells from leaves to – storage organs, e.g. roots – growing regions, e.g. shoot tips.
- Minerals transported by xylem dissolved in water.

GREEN PLANTS AS ORGANISMS

Minerals and plant health

Nitrates

- Essential for synthesis of DNA.
- Essential for the **synthesis of protein**.
- Remember **glucose** contains the elements carbon, hydrogen and oxygen.
- **Proteins** contain these three elements together with nitrogen.
- Protein is needed to make **membranes, enzymes and chlorophyll.**

Nitrate deficiency
- Causes poor growth in plants.
- Little protein made – no new cells – proteins are a vital part of cell membranes – enzymes that control cells are made of protein.
- Plants compensate – produce new leaves – they have to move whatever nitrogen they have to growth areas so the older leaves become yellow and die off.

Summary: **Plants that are stunted in growth with yellow older leaves are nitrate or nitrogen deficient.**

Potassium

- Needed for the **synthesis** of **some enzymes**.
- Cannot synthesise chemicals and produce energy.

Potassium deficiency
- Growth is limited – not as badly affected as in nitrate deficiency.
- Photosynthesis and respiration impaired – plant will have many problems.
- Young leaves are yellow as **chlorophyll** (green pigment) synthesis is restricted – enzyme problems.
- Leaves eventually turn green as the plant moves resources to compensate areas of cell death due to lack of enzymes.

Summary: **Potassium deficiency causes yellow leaves with dead spots.**

Learn the 3 mineral summaries!

Phosphate

- Needed to **synthesise some proteins** but not all – also DNA.
- If essential proteins cannot be made – growth will be affected.
- Phosphate has **an important role** in **photosynthesis** and **respiration**.

Phosphate deficiency
- Root growth is severely affected – roots are short with few side roots.
- Young leaves produced that are purple in colour.
- Chlorophyll not synthesised properly – enzyme problems.

Summary: **Phosphate deficiency causes stunted root growth and purple younger leaves.**

Plant hormones

Phototropism

- **Shoots** grow towards light – away from gravity.
- **Roots** grow towards water and gravity – away from light.
- Shoots bend towards light because the hormone auxin causes lengthening of cells.
- Shoot tip produces **auxin** – this moves back down the plant stem.
- If light is from one side only auxin is transferred to the shaded side.
- This side lengthens more – the shoot bends over – **towards the light.**

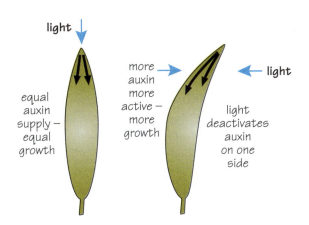

Hormones – **control plant growth.**

Roots

- Rooting powders – used to promote the growth of stem cuttings.
- Hormone promotes the growth of healthy roots on the cut stem.
- Many plants produced very quickly by promoting root growth on many stem cuttings.

Shoots

- Shoot tips produce hormones that inhibit the growth of side shoots.
- This promotes increase in length.
- Removal of tip – side shoots grow – plants become bushy – NB. cutting hedges.

Fruit

- Hormones sprayed on flowers – causes the formation of fruit.
- Fruit has not been fertilised and is seedless.
- Fruit is also bigger than normal as energy has not been used to produce seeds.
- Hormones also sprayed to speed up or slow down fruit development – on the tree or after the fruit is picked – farmer will be able to produce the crop at the best time for the climate and the market.

Weedkillers

- Growth hormones sprayed onto plants – plants grow too quickly, run short of energy and die.
- Hormones are selective for certain types of plant – weedkiller works from within – when plant dies the hormone should be broken down in the soil.

Benefits of hormones

- Production of many new plants, identical to parent, by cuttings.
- Development of seedless fruit.
- Selective weedkillers that do not pollute the soil.

Problems with hormones

- If plant hormones aren't broken down in the soil – enter the food chain – could cause problems – some may behave as female hormones – fish and alligators in Florida lake have been found to have both male and female organs in the same animal – investigating the link to pesticides (DDT, etc.) and herbicides (weedkillers).

You may need to discuss this in the form of a short essay!

Transport and water relations – transpiration

- **Plants absorb most of their water through root hair cells.**
- Plants lose water through their leaves – this is dependent on the structure of the leaves.
- Water evaporates from spongy mesophyll cells → enters the spaces in the leaf → diffuses towards stomata pores → evaporates from the leaf.
- Water that is lost from leaves is replaced by water from the roots.

Copy diagrams and label them from memory.

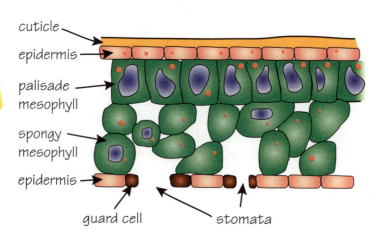

- **Water flows from roots through the stem and to leaves in xylem vessels.**
- This movement of water is called the transpiration stream – fastest on hot, windy, dry, sunny days – slows down on cold, wet and dark days.
- **Minerals are also transported through the plant by xylem vessels.**

Water regulation in the plant

- Stomata – holes in the underside of leaves – restrict the loss of water.
- Guard cells – special cells that open or close stomata.

Daylight/plant has a lot of water:
- Photosynthesising as fast as possible.
- Stomata are wide open for efficient photosynthesis, so transpiration occurs at the maximum rate.

Plant is short of water/dark:
- Stomata close – restricts water loss.
- Photosynthesis also slows down or stops.

Plants that live in dry climates are adapted to restrict water loss by:
- Having thicker cuticle – prevents water evaporating from upper leaf surface.
- Reducing their leaves to spikes (cacti).
- Having hairs on leaves.
- Having stomata in sunken pits.

Osmosis - explanation

Plant cells absorb or lose water by osmosis depending upon the concentration of solutes in their cell cytoplasm and vacuole:

Learn your teacher's definition of osmosis.

- **Gaining water** – dilute outside cell – concentrated inside – water enters cell by osmosis – the cell swells.
- **Turgid** – cell full of water – turgid cells very important to all plants – water gives the cells support.
- **Losing water** – concentrated outside cell – more dilute inside – water leaves cell by osmosis – the cell shrinks.
- **Flaccid** – when only a little water is lost – plant wilts.
- **Plasmolysed** – loss of too much water – cytoplasm shrinks away from the cell wall – plant dies.

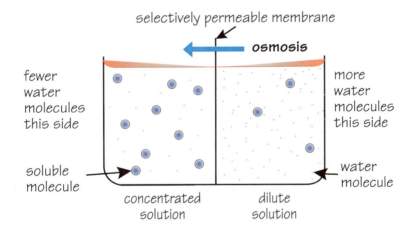

Summary
Think of a plant cell as a football (the leather case is like the cellulose cell wall and the rubber inner tube the vacuole). The more air you blow into a football the harder it becomes (water entering the vacuole makes a plant cell **turgid**). If air is let out of the football it becomes soft (water leaving the plant vacuole makes the cell soft – **plasmolysed**).

Remember that a low concentration has a lot of water with not much dissolved in it - the low refers to what is dissolved not the water. A high concentration has a lot of dissolved chemicals - the water is dissolving them - so there is little water left to move by osmosis.

GREEN PLANTS AS ORGANISMS

65

Questions

1 What is the green pigment in plants called and where in the cell is it found?

2 Which cells in the leaf are specially adapted for photosynthesis?

3 What is the name of the cells in a plant that transport water?

4 What is the name of the tissue in a plant that transports food?

5 What is the name of the tissue in a plant that transports minerals?

6 In which conditions would photosynthesis be greatest?

7 In which conditions would photosynthesis be at its lowest?

8 In which conditions would transpiration be very high?

9 In which conditions would transpiration be very low?

10 Which time of year is photosynthesis greatest?

11 Which time of year will trees produce the largest xylem?

12 What is the name of the process that describes how glucose leaves and enters a plant cell?

13 By what process does water leave and enter a cell?

14 What word describes a cell full of water?

15 What word describes a cell that is lacking in water?

16 Which mineral deficiency causes very poor growth in plants?

17 Which mineral deficiency causes young leaves to be purple in plants?

18 Which mineral deficiency causes leaves to turn yellow?

19 Which mineral deficiency causes dead spots on leaves?

20 Which mineral deficiency causes stunted root growth?

21 Which mineral deficiency causes the plant's older leaves to turn yellow?

22 How do plant shoots respond to light?

23 How do plant shoots respond to gravity?

Answers

Life processes and cell activity

1 botany 2 zoology 3 sensitivity 4 respiration 5 excretion
6 elimination or egestion 7 reproduction 8 growth 9 oxygen
10 respiration 11 respiration/produce energy 12 MRS FERG 13 cytoplasm
14 nucleus 15 cellulose cell wall 16 chloroplast 17 vacuole 18 tissue
19 organ 20 system 21 organism 22 vacuole, cellulose cell wall, chlorophyll
23 cell 24 organ 25 organ 26 movement of molecules from area of high
concentration to area of low concentration 27 movement of molecules using energy
from respiration

Humans as organisms

1 carbohydrate, protein, fat 2 peristalsis 3 kills germs and creates the correct
medium for gastric protease 4 emulsifies fats, increases their surface area and
helps neutralise stomach acid 5 digests protein to amino acids 6 right ventricle
7 left ventricle 8 withstand high blood pressure and maintain blood pressure
9 keep blood travelling the right way, prevent backflow 10 carry oxygen 11 urea,
carbon dioxide, any food, hormones 12 alveoli 13 aerobic 14 anaerobic
15 stimulus – receptor – co-ordinator – effector – response 16 ligament, capsule or
synovial membrane, synovial fluid or cartilage 17 insulin 18 glucagon/adrenaline
19 FSH 20 LH 21 broken down to urea by liver 22 more permeable to water,
water reabsorbed back into blood, concentrated urine produced 23 Fallopian tube
24 fourteen

Variation, inheritance and evolution

1 46 2 genes 3 DNA 4 23 5 living things have potential to overproduce,
population numbers remain constant over long periods of time, all living things show
variation, some types of variation are inherited 6 XY 7 extinct 8 homozygous
recessive 9 heterozygous 10 heterozygous 11 homozygous dominant
12 homozygous recessive 13 fossils 14 natural selection 15 over 3,000
million years 16 clones 17 selective breeding 18 mitosis 19 meiosis
20 genetic engineering 21 ultra violet, X-ray, gamma

Microbes, disease and biotechnology

1 microbe that decays dead matter 2 protozoa/protoctists 3 rabies
4 microbe that causes disease 5 mosquito 6 canning, UHT, pasteurisation,
drying, freezing, salting, syrup (high sugar), irradiation – any 5 7 chemical that kills
microbes within the body 8 using vaccination to become immune to disease
9 live attenuated, dead, protein coat/surface antigen, toxoid molecule, genetic
engineering producing viral antigen in bacteria 10 chemical that kills microbes
outside the body 11 chemical that kills microbes on non-living materials
12 a) pacemakers/new valves b) kidney machines c) replacement joints
13 fermentation 14 fermentation of animal droppings or waste sugars
15 fermentation in a sealed vessel – left to grow for a set time 16 fermentation in a
vessel that allows continuous removal of substrate over several days/weeks
17 biological washing powders 18 single cell protein – produced from algae or fungi

Living things and their environment

1 nitrate/phosphate   2 'building brick' of all molecules of life   3 to make proteins
4 nitrate   5 plants   6 other animals   7 denitrifyers   8 nitrogen fixers
9 ammonia   10 nitrate, carbon dioxide, water   11 six legs, wings, three body parts
12 gill filaments collapse/stick together, not supported by water, lose large surface
area   13 carbon dioxide   14 carbon dioxide   15 0.03%   16 nitrogen fixers
17 sulphur dioxide   18 carbon dioxide and methane   19 carbon dioxide   20
sulphur dioxide and carbon dioxide   21 acid rain   22 cyanide

Green plants as organisms

1 chlorophyll – in chloroplasts   2 palisade mesophyll   3 xylem   4 phloem
5 xylem   6 bright light, warm, high CO_2 levels   7 dark/cloudy, cold, low CO_2 levels
8 warm, windy, dry, light   9 cold, wet, still, dark   10 summer   11 summer
12 diffusion   13 osmosis   14 turgid   15 plasmolysed   16 nitrate
17 phosphate   18 potassium/nitrate   19 potassium   20 phosphate
21 nitrate   22 grow towards   23 grow away

Index

adrenaline 23
aerobic and anaerobic
    respiration 16–17
air composition 15–16,
    49–50
antibiotics 44
arthritis 25
arthropods 55
assimilation in plants 61

bacteria 37, 42, 46, 57
biogas 44–5
biotechnology 41–6
blood 12–14
    circulation and vessels 12
    groups 13
    sugar 20–1
breathing 14–16

carbon cycle 54
cell division 6, 32
cell membranes 7
cells 4–7, 12–13
central nervous system
    17–19
chromosomes 27–31
classification of organisms
    55
cloning 33
competition 48–9

defence against disease 13,
    38, 40–1
deforestation 50
diet 9, 51
diffusion 7
digestion 9–11
diseases 28–32, 37–9
DNA 30
drugs 25

ecosystems 53
energy sources 51
environment 27, 48–50
enzymes 10, 42, 45–6
evolution 34–5
eye 18

fermentation 43–5
fertilisers 49–50
food
    biotechnology 42
    chains and pyramids 51–2
    poisoning and spoilage 40
    production 42, 46, 55
    tests   9
fossils 34
• fungi 37, 42, 44, 46, 57

genetic
    diseases 28–32
    engineering 32, 45, 53
genetics 6, 27–35
greenhouse effect 50

heart 11
homeostasis 22–4
hormones 20–2, 63–4
human effects on the
    environment 49–50
hygiene 41

immunity 13–14
invertebrates 55

kidneys 22–3

life characteristics 4
Louis Pasteur 38–9

malaria 39
meiosis 6, 32
menstrual cycle 20–1
methane 44–5, 50
microbes 13, 37–46, 51, 56,
    59
minerals 61–2
mitosis 6, 32
mutations 31

nervous system 17–19
neurons 17–18
nitrogen cycle 54
nutrition 9

organs 5, 22–3
osmosis 7, 65

penicillin 44
photosynthesis 48, 54,
    59–62, 64–5
plant growth 61–4
plants 5–7, 48, 54–7,
    59–65
pollution 49–51
populations 48–9
proteins 46, 54
    synthesis 31
protoctists and protozoa
    37, 51

radiation 31
reflex action 19
reproduction 4, 19–20, 33
respiration 4, 14–17, 50, 54

selection of organisms 33–5,
    53
senses 18
sex chromosomes 28
sex linked diseases 29–30,
    32
skeleton 24
synovial joint 24
systems 5, 10, 14

temperature control 24
tissue culture 33
tissues 5
transpiration 64–5
transplants 41

vaccines 38, 40–1
variation between organisms
    27
vertebrates 56
viruses 38, 57

water 7, 48–9
water regulation 22–3, 64–5
white blood cells 13

NOTES

These pages can be used for your own notes

NOTES

Success or your money back

Letts' market leading series GCSE Revision Notes gives you everything you need for exam success. We're so confident that they're the best revision books you can buy that if you don't make the grade we will give you your money back!

HERE'S HOW IT WORKS

Register the Letts GCSE Revision Notes you buy by writing to us within 28 days of purchase with the following information:

- Name
- Address
- Postcode
- Subject of GCSE Revision Notes book bought – please include your till receipt or school name and address and subject teacher
- Probable tier you will enter

To make a **claim**, compare your results to the grades below. If any of your grades qualify for a refund, make a claim by writing to us within 28 days of getting your results, enclosing a copy of your original exam slip. If you do not register, you won't be able to make a claim after you receive your results.

CLAIM IF...

You're a Higher Tier student and get a grade D or below

You're an Intermediate Tier student and get a grade E or below

You're a Foundation Tier student and get a grade F or below

You're a Scottish Standard Grade Student taking Credit and General Level exams and get a grade 4 or below

This offer is not open to Scottish Standard Grade students sitting Foundation Level exams.

Registration and claim address:

Letts Success or Your Money Back Offer, Letts Educational, Aldine Place, London W12 8AW

TERMS AND CONDITIONS

1 Applies to the Letts GCSE Revision Notes series only
2 Registration of purchases must be received by Letts Educational within 28 days of the purchase date
3 Registration must be accompanied by a valid till receipt
4 All money back claims must be received by Letts Educational within 28 days of receiving exam results
5 All claims must be accompanied by a letter stating the claim and a copy of the relevant exam results slip
6 Claims will be invalid if they do not match with the original registered subjects
7 Letts Educational reserves the right to seek confirmation of the level of entry of the claimant

8 Responsibility cannot be accepted for lost, delayed or damaged applications, or applications received outside of the stated registration / claim timescales
9 Proof of posting will not be accepted as proof of delivery
10 Offer only available to GCSE students studying within the UK
11 SUCCESS OR YOUR MONEY BACK is promoted by Letts Educational, Aldine Place, London W12 8AW
12 Registration indicates a complete acceptance of these rules
13 Illegible entries will be disqualified
14 In all matters, the decision of Letts Educational will be final and no correspondence will be entered into

---

Letts Educational
Aldine Place
London W12 8AW
Tel: 020 8740 2266
Fax: 020 8743 8451
email: mail@lettsed.co.uk
website: www.letts-education.com

Every effort has been made to trace copyright holders and obtain their permission for the use of copyright material. The authors and publishers will gladly receive information enabling them to rectify any error or omission in subsequent editions.

First published 1998
Reprinted 1998, 1999
New edition 1999
This edition 2000

Text © John Dobson 2000
Editorial and design by Hart McLeod, Cambridge

All our Rights Reserved. No part of this publication may be reproduced, stored in a retrieval system, or transmitted, in any form or by any means, electronic, mechanical, photocopying, recording or otherwise, without the prior permission of Letts Educational.

British Library Cataloguing in Publication Data
A CIP record for this book is available from the British Library.

ISBN 1 84085 473 1

Printed in Italy

Letts Educational Limited is a division of Granada Learning Limited, part of the Granada Media Group.